BEIJING WOMEN ORGANIZING FOR CHANGE

Nordic Institute of Asian Studies
Recent NIAS Reports

A full list of NIAS publications is available on request or may be viewed online (see copyright page for contact details).

BEIJING WOMEN ORGANIZING FOR CHANGE

A New Wave of the Chinese Women's Movement

Cecilia Milwertz

NIAS
Press

Nordic Institute of Asian Studies
NIAS Report series, no. 40

First published in 2002 by NIAS Press
Reprinted in 2003
Nordic Institute of Asian Studies
Leifsgade 33, DK–2300 Copenhagen S, Denmark
tel: (+45) 3532 9501 • fax: (+45) '3532 9549
E–mail: books@nias.ku.dk • Website: http://www.niaspress.dk/

Typesetting by NIAS Press
Produced by Bookchase
Printed and bound in Great Britain

British Library Cataloguing in Publication Data
Milwertz, Cecilia Nathansen
    Beijing women organizing for change : a new wave of the Chinese women's
    movement. - (NIAS reports ; no. 40)
    1.Feminism - China - Beijing
    I.Title II.Nordic Institute of Asian Studies
    305.4'2'0951156

ISBN 87-87062-72-0

The hard part of dedicated social movement involvement lies in the recognition that it is the persistent tapping – sometimes a hammer, sometimes a feather – that leaves a mark. And it is through this process, a series of marks, that a new cultural reality is born.
– Barbara Ryan 1992

Regardless of what we can or cannot do in Chinese society, if everyone feels that we can't do anything, then we will never succeed. We have to work hard. We have to slowly work towards our goals. We will fail along the way – but in the end we will succeed.
– Beijing activist, December 2000

This volume is dedicated to the persistent tapping of women's movement activists in China.

CONTENTS

LIST OF FIGURES

PREFACE AND ACKNOWLEDGEMENTS

International interest in women's organizing in China was especially strong in connection with the United Nations Fourth World Conference on Women held in Beijing in 1995. I recall the exasperated e-mail sigh – 'so many of these women's organizations and civil society projects have come across my desk!' – expressed by a friend working with a donor organization in Beijing when I sent her a draft project description that year. Since she knew and worked with popular women's organizations, she watched in frustration as interested, even fascinated, but also often somewhat detached academic and media spectators, investigators and visitors imposed a drain on activist resources. However much they appreciate the attention afforded them (and need the funding that may follow upon this attention), activists have always found continuous visits by journalists, academics, students, donor organization representatives, politicians and their spouses and many others, whatever the main focus of their interest, relatively time-consuming. Though the stream of visits may have diminished since 1995, I hope that this book will be read by those who plan to visit the Jinglun Family Centre, the Maple Women's Psychological Counselling Centre and the Migrant Women's Club, and that in so doing they will be better prepared than I was when I started my interviews, thereby taking up less of the activists' precious time, perhaps asking more qualified questions and increasing the mutual benefit of the visits.

This book developed over the course of conversations and interviews with many scholars and activists in China, and I thank every one of them. I owe special thanks to Professor Qi Wenying at Beijing University who first introduced me, in 1992, to some of the people I met. As I proceeded, the effect snowballed, and I was introduced to more and more activists. Thanks go, first of all, to the three directors of the main organizations in this book – Wang Xingjuan, Chen Yiyun and Xie

ix

Lihua - and to Wu Qing, co-initiator of the Migrant Women's Club, and to the many other activists in each of the three organizations and the other organizations, groups and networks that have offered their valuable time and hospitality.

In 1996 Lisa Stearns and I wrote a chapter on women's organizing in China for a Norwegian book, but on the request of the director of one of the organizations about which we had written, we never published it, since for her organization, it was politically a particularly sensitive time. My thanks go to Lisa for her friendship, her generous sharing of friends and knowledge, and for thoughts and even wordings in this volume which originate from our joint chapter.

Thanks are also due to the institutions that have supported my research. Two visits to China (one in September 1994 and one in August–September 1995, to prepare for and attend, respectively, the Women's Conference NGO Forum) were sponsored by the Danish women's NGO, KULU – Women and Development. A three-week visit in May 1996 was funded by a travel grant from the Nordic Institute of Asian Studies (NIAS) and an exchange agreement between NIAS and the Chinese Academy of Social Sciences. All visits since 1996 have been hosted by the Institute of Sociology, the Chinese Academy of Social Sciences, where Zhao Kebin especially has been enormously helpful. Two visits in 1997 and 1998 were made possible by grants from the British Academy. The remaining visits in 1997 and 1998 were funded by the European Science Foundation during my affiliation to the Institute for Chinese Studies at Oxford University as European Science Foundation Research Fellow from 1996 to 1999. I am particularly grateful to Professor Glen Dudbridge for his support during the years I spent at Oxford University. This volume is a result of my research there. It is linked to the book *Chinese Women Organizing – Cadres, Feminists, Muslims, Queers* (Hsiung, Jaschok and Milwertz with Chanh 2001), proceedings of the Workshop 'Women Organizing in China' held at Oxford University in July 1999. The titles of the two books are perhaps confusingly similar. This reflects the fact that they were created simultaneously and that both address women's organizing for social change from the grassroots level upward. In terms of content, the two books do not overlap; on the contrary, they supplement each other.

The present book was finalized after I returned to the Nordic Institute of Asian Studies (NIAS) in September 1999. I thank NIAS' librarians Marianne Espenhain Nielsen, Inga-Lill Blomqvist and Per Hansen for their help and the publishing unit, especially my desk editor Liz Bramsen, for warm support and patience. My grateful thanks go to colleagues who have read and commented on draft versions of chapters of the book or helped in other ways – Feng Yuan, Ge Youli, Geir Helgesen, Maria Jaschok, Liu Dongxiao, Min Dongchao, Nicola Piper, Suzanne Plesner, Hatla Thelle, Qi Wang, and Zhang Naihua – and to Solveig Bergman and the Nordic Women's Movements and Internationalization Network. The work of Network members, shared at our meetings, has been a strong source of inspiration. Finally, I wish to thank my family and friends, who sustained me in personally turbulent times.

C.M.
Copenhagen

ABBREVIATIONS

ACWF	All China Women's Federation
CASS	Chinese Academy of Social Sciences
CASW	China Association of Social Workers
CSWS	Chinese Society for Women's Studies
CWLSLS	Centre for Women's Law Studies and Legal Services
EMW	East Meets West Feminist Translation Group
JFC	Jinglun Family Centre
MWC	Migrant Women's Club
MWPCC	Maple Women's Psychological Counselling Centre
Sida	Swedish International Development Cooperation Agency
WRI	Women's Research Institute

1 Introduction

Since the 1980s a new historical phase of the women's liberation movement in China has developed. An important aspect of this evolution has been the rise and activity of various popular women's organizations (Liu Jinxiu 1991: 106). These organizations emerged when women began to organize again on their own initiative to support vulnerable social groups, to create social change and to challenge gender-based inequalities in society. For many years prior to this development, 'there was a top-down women's movement in China, initiated by the Party-led ACWF. It was sarcastically dubbed a "move women movement" instead of a "women's movement"' (Feng Yuan 2000: 1).

Three of these 'popular women's organizations' in Beijing – the Women's Research Institute[1] (which became the Maple Women's Psychological Counselling Center), the Jinglun Family Centre and the Migrant Women's Club are the focus of this book. In comparison to numerous other secular and religious women's organizations, groups and networks that have emerged or re-emerged in many parts of the People's Republic of China in the 1980s and 1990s, these three organizations and their formidable directors, Wang Xingjuan, Chen Yiyun and Xie Lihua, have relatively often been the centre of the attention from Western European and North American media, donor

---

1. The Women's Research Institute (Funü yanjiusuo) is distinct from the All China Women's Federation-Women's Studies Institute of China (Quanguo fulian funü yanjiusuo).

1

organizations and academia. Internationally distributed English-language media have reported on the work of these three organizations since their very beginning in the late 1980s to early 1990s. *Newsweek* carried an article on the psychological counselling work of sociologist Chen Yiyun as early as 1990, several years before she set up the Jinglun Family Centre (Privat 1990).[2]

Reports for international donor organizations engaged in gender and development programmes in China, such as the Swedish International Development Cooperation Agency (Sida) and the US Ford Foundation (Fennel and Jeffery 1992, Stearns 1996, Rabb 1997, Croll 1998), and academic studies have also noted the role of or engaged in studies of one or several of these three organizations (Croll 1995, Howell 1997a, Wang Zheng 1997, Wesoky 1998, Cornue 1999 and Milwertz 2000a, 2000b). This focus has not always pleased authorities in China, and in 1995 the attention that the Women's Research Institute received from non-Chinese media and top level politicians from Europe and the United States of America in connection with the United Nations Fourth World Conference on Women, held in Beijing, very nearly led to closure of the Institute.

Feminist organizing is often marginalized in both Chinese and Western society, and the interest that these organizations have generated in Western media, donor organizations and politicians is in large part due to their existence and activities being viewed as expressions of the development of civil society and a transformation towards a democratic society in China. As in the former Soviet Union and Eastern Europe (Racioppi and See 1995), the transition in China from planned to market economy has had numerous negative political and economic impacts – especially on the lives of women. These developments have simultaneously given rise to opportunities for the establishment of a plurality of women's organizations. New forms of women's organizations in post-Mao China have been scrutinized with a view to analysing their existence as signs of the development of a less politically controlled relationship between party-state and society and the emergence of civil society, public space or a public sphere. China scholars have defined the women's organizations and women's studies which have been set up since the mid-1980s as a social movement associated with features such as autonomy and grassroots initiative on the one hand and, on the other hand, as lacking the core

2. See also Burton 1990, Walker 1993, Brittain and Jakobsen 1995, MacLeod 1997, Elliott 1998, Forney 1998.

characteristics of such a movement. In the UK, Lin Chun hailed women's organizing activities in post-Mao China as 'the first autonomous social movement ever to flourish in our country' – a movement that is politically significant in terms of the role that it plays in creating and institutionalizing a public sphere as the basis for development of 'a democratic citizenship' (Lin Chun 1995a: 60, Lin Chun 1996: 286). Similarly, in the USA Wang Zheng defined the women's studies initiated in the 1980s by the All China Women's Federation (ACWF) and academic institutions in many cities as 'a movement of research' that '… is one of the most significant developments in contemporary China because it represents the first time in Chinese history that women have initiated a national movement' (Wang Zheng 1997: 146). On a somewhat more restrained note, which is perhaps due to the particular reference to professional women's organizations, Gordon White, Jude Howell and Shang Xiaoyuan state in their study of civil society in China that

> As these organizations meet only intermittently and face financial constraints in organizing activities, their capacity to become fora to articulate women's interests and increase their participation in society is limited. As with other associations in the 'incorporated' sector, most of these women's organizations also reflect an attempt by the state to keep control of newly emerging interests and channel them into a body that can be monitored and contained. *For those looking for the development of a genuine feminist movement in China, with grass roots, voluntary women's groups, the wait is clearly going to be long.* (White, Howell and Shang 1996: 96, emphasis added)

Is there, then, a new women's movement in China? Or have donor organizations, journalists, politicians and academics merely character-ized a few new organizations, which perhaps looked somewhat familiar to women's NGOs in other parts of the world, as signs of a new movement and nascent civil society, simply in order to confirm that a development they aspired to was actually materializing? The present volume introduces the establishment and activities of three prominent Beijing women's organizations – the Women's Research Institute/Maple Women's Psychological Counselling Centre, the Jinglun Family Centre and the Migrant Women's Club. The aim is to contribute to an understanding of women's organizing in the 1980s and 1990s. Why, how and by whom were these organizations set up? What aims do they have, and how have they worked to attain them? The central argument is that the three organizations are actors in a new wave of the continuing Chinese women's movement. The practice of the three organizations constitutes part of a formative phase of a new social movement wave based on popular initiative in Beijing and beyond. As already mentioned, several studies have defined women's studies and other organizing activities by women in China in the 1980s and 1990s as a new women's movement (Lin Chun 1995a, Wang Zheng 1997, Wesoky 1999, Naihua Zhang 1995). However, vagueness in defining 'movement' and variations in defining the movement as including or excluding the All China Women's Federation (ACWF) adds to the confusion in understanding the nature of these new types of organizing in relation to the long term women's movement in China.

I shall adopt political scientist Drude Dahlerups's definition of social movement and of social movement waves to understand the new forms of organizing in China.[3] Thus, a social movement is '*a conscious, collective* activity to promote *social change*, with some degree of organization and with the commitment and active participation of members or activists as its main resource' (Dahlerup 1986: 218). Dahlerup adds three characteristics to this main definition. First, '[t]o be termed a "social movement", the activity must represent certain fundamental interests, must last for some time, and must have a certain size and several component parts. It is characterized by a combination of spontaneity and organization.' Second, a social movement represents 'interests that, by definition, are not incorporated into routine politics. Social movements are marginal to the political decision-making processes. A social movement represents a protest against the established norms and values, and usually includes an attack on the power structure itself. Because it does not possess institutionalized power, it often uses direct actions and disruptive tactics. In this, the social movement differs from the routine politics of interest organizations'. Third, a social movement consists of 'an entity of activities by organizations, groups and followers who share a commitment to a common cause.' (Ibid.). In Chapter Five, I shall argue that organizing by women in Beijing qualifies as social movement activism, even though it does not fit neatly and precisely into this definition. It does not, for example, apply 'direct actions and disruptive tactics'. On the contrary, the movement applies non-disruptive modes of action, since these are effective in the Chinese

---

3. For a critical discussion of the usefulness of applying a theory of waves to the study of women's movements, see Lønnå 2000.

political context. Movement waves are characterized first, by the establishment of many new feminist organizations and groups; second, by extensive debate within the movement and publicly; and third, by the fact that the ideas of the movement are making an impact in terms of new laws and/or changes in the discourse on women in society (Dahlerup 1998: 122). In her study of India, Gail Omvedt defines a new phase of the women's movement as characterized by 'new energies, new themes, new forms of struggle'. These are 'new' in that women themselves 'through the ideologies they generate, define their exploitation and oppression, the system that generates these, and the way to end this exploitation and oppression, in "new" terms' thus yielding new feminist articulations (Omvedt 1993: 77). Based on Dahlerup's definition of new waves within a continuous movement, this volume will analyse activities and modes of action applied by the three Beijing organizations in their effort to effectively address social issues and create social change. The emphasis of the analysis is on 'the transformative intent and impact of feminist organizations' (Ferree and Martin 1995: 7), in other words, on the process, context, content and culture of organizing rather than on the structure and institutional relationships of the three organizations. Structural relationships of these three organizations to the All China Women's Federation and other party-state institutions are addressed to the degree that these have an impact on organizational practice.[4] The new phase of the movement wave is characterized by the innovation – within the political context of the People's Republic of China – of women organizing on their own initiative. Women have set up groups, organizations and networks, and they have organized activities in the name of these. They have found office space and meeting places. They have sought funding. They have made their voices heard in the media and through recommendations to policy-makers. Less visibly, the wave is characterized by innovative understandings, thinking and knowledge, which form the basis for challenging dominant discourses on women and gender issues. Finally, the movement wave is characterized by innovative internal organizational practices.

---

4. Liu Dongxiao 1999 provides a fine analysis of institutional heterogeneity in terms of *'tizhi nei'* [inside the institution] and *'tizhi wai'* [outside the institution]. This analysis shapes popular organizations with a dual nature which reflects both the influences of the communist state and limited socioeconomic pluralism.

Dahlerup's wave theory, which was developed on the basis of studies of Western women's movements – primarily the Danish women's movement – posits that 'so many common features can be identified between the older and the newer feminist movements, that it makes sense to maintain that the feminist movements that have emerged since the 1960s, are not a totally new phenomenon in history, but represent *a new wave of an old movement*'. A new wave represents 'a new type of feminism' and 'a new strong wave of mobilization after a period of more quiet feminist work' (Dahlerup 2000: 11). The present study does not seek to define the exact links between current organizing and earlier periods of organizing – this would require additional studies. However, the new wave is seen as a continuation of older movements. There is a historical continuity of women's collective social protest. It links the current movement both to gender equality policies in the People's Republic prior to the 1980s and to the May Fourth movement at the beginning of the twentieth century, when Western feminism was actively deployed and appropriated by groups in China in the pursuit of their interests and rights (see Wang Zheng 1999).

The new wave includes organizations, activists and activities situated both within and outside the structural framework of the ACWF and other party-state institutions. As noted by Liu Jinxiu, and cited at the very beginning of this chapter, the rise of popular women's organizations is *one aspect* of the development of a new phase of the Chinese women's movement. The formation of the movement wave, in which the three popular women's organizations have been active participants, is not limited to the activities of these three organizations; nor it is limited to the capital. Popular *organizing* (that is, organizing on the popular level, and *not* the organizations themselves) has played an active and important role in forming a new wave of the Chinese women's movement. Other actors within this process of organizing include centres of women's and gender studies and activists placed within institutions such as the ACWF and the Trade Union Women Workers' Department. This study has not investigated and cannot determine to what degree these two and other party-state led institutions have been actively involved in forming the new wave of the women's movement in the sense of initiating debates and social change based on innovative knowledge and practices. It is clear, however, that the new wave has been formed by collective organizing across institutions, and has included active participants from within party-state institutions.

Organizing for social change has set a particular process of change in motion, in which activists challenge and oppose culturally constructed and generally accepted gender ideologies and practices. This movement demands the recognition of various forms of gender inequality and works to create a change in attitudes, understandings and practices concerning gender issues. The present book reflects a change of focus that took place in the course of a study made of the Women's Research Institute, the Jinglun Family Centre and the Migrant Women's Club. Initially, my interest was directed at each of these three organizations as an individual expression of civil society, broadly defined as a sphere or space which is structurally and operationally separate and autonomous from the party-state. Gradually, the focus shifted towards several women's organizations, groups and networks as parts of a larger collective women's movement. Apart from reflecting a quantitative inclusion of a larger number of organizations, groups and networks, the main implication of this shift was a qualitative change in the theoretical approach.

The theoretical premises of this study fall in line with recognition by China-scholars that civil society in China does not replicate a binary state–civil society opposition, but is characterized by what has been termed a 'peculiar blend of private, public and state' (Perry 1995). The incorporation of a wider range of women's activities is based on an understanding of organizing and 'organization' as 'a generic term, pointing out capacity to accomplish goals through collective action within a structure' (Bryant 1985, cited in Rosander 1997: 103), and on a concept of civil society which is defined not negatively, in opposition to the state, but positively, within the context of the ideas and practices through which cooperation and trust are established in social life. This focus corresponds to the call – from anthropologists in particular – for a shift in the debate on civil society away from formal structures and organizations towards an investigation of beliefs, values and everyday practices (Hann 1996). This shift in focus derives from the recognition that one of the principal modes of action applied by the new organizations is based on utilizing personal networks that cut across institutions regardless of their structural links to the party-state. When values, beliefs and practice are viewed as the core of civil society, then it is not the individual organization that is of primary importance. On the contrary, civil society is constituted by the values and practice of the collective women's movement, of which the individual organization is but one part.

Following Drude Dahlerup's definition of a social movement, the 1980s–1990s phase of the women's movement in China can be seen to consist of 'an entity of activities by organizations, groups and followers who share a commitment to a common cause'. In terms of understanding the Chinese women's movement – in which there are many fluid links between activists and activities situated within and outside the formal structures of the ACWF and other party-state institutions – this concise definition contains three important elements. First, that *activities* rather than structure of organizations are emphasized. Second, that these activities are carried out not by one organization but by a collective of several *organizations, groups and followers*, or by what Suzanne Staggenborg (1995: 345) defines as 'a social movement community'. Third, that regardless of whether or not individuals involved are attached to one, several or no organizations, they are primarily characterized by *sharing a commitment to a common cause*. The thing that binds activists and their activities together to constitute the current wave of the Chinese women's movement is the combination of a collective mode of questioning and challenging existing practice and a collective commitment to action aimed at emancipation through the substitution of better practices for unequal and discriminating ones.

This study reflects a shift in focus from the structure of separate women's organizations to the values of shared ideology, shared awareness of gender inequality, shared definitions of gender inequality as illegitimate and an engagement in common action for change. This shift away from a focus on the opposition between new forms of organizing and the party-state makes it possible also to acknowledge and analyse the fact that the activities of the women's movement not only aim at protest against the party-state and its policies, but also at cooperation with the party-state in addressing practices such as domestic violence in society. I adopt an understanding of civil society as 'a community bonded and empowered by its collective determination to resist, on the one hand, excessive constraints of the society and, on the other, excessive regulations by the state' (Chamberlain 1993: 207), in which community is used in the sense of widely shared beliefs and attitudes. This view of civil society provides an alternative understanding of the various forms of cooperation between the new and the old women's organizations. One can go beyond regarding the development in China from the existence of one single party-state-initiated women's organization to many women's organizations as a question mainly of these new organizations' dependence upon, incorporation by or opposition to the old women's organization and the party-state as such. These aspects, of course, still need to be considered. However, with a non-oppositional definition of civil society and a focus on the cognitive praxis of new forms of organizing, it becomes possible to view both new organizations and elements of the All China Women's Federation and other party-state institutions as parts of one collective phase of the women's movement.

The new wave of the movement is characterized by the strength of change and innovation – of feminist transformative practice. What started out as a reaction to discrimination against women made visible by economic reforms has developed into various interpretations of and activism against gender inequalities. One of the defining features of the wave is the openness to discussion and reinterpretation. The wave is not static – it is characterized by its continuous transformation of thinking and practice. Rather than defining feminism normatively, it is viewed as 'a transformational process' (Bhasin and Kahn cited in Margolis 1993: 384). The new wave of the movement – or parts of it – may not initially have been feminist in the sense of challenging women's subordinate positions in society and working towards what Maxine Molyneux has defined as 'strategic gender interests' (Molyneux 1985, Moser 1993). However, the very process of organizing has developed various types of transformational feminisms.[5] Recent acknowledgement of diversity in women's activism and feminism has demonstrated the importance of going beyond articulated gender interests to include many forms of activism as expressions of feminism, even when they have not been explicitly defined as such by participants themselves (Gluck 1998). In order to fully appreciate and include local forms and definitions of organization towards social change and full citizenship, Molyneux's (1985) and Moser's (1993) definitions of practical and strategic gender interests are applied as a tool for operationalizing women's activism, but the analysis also goes beyond these. A broad working definition of feminism as '[w]omen's groups (including formal and informal committees, subcommittees and caucuses) organized for change, whose agendas AND/OR actions challenge women's subordinate [or disadvantaged] status in the society at large (external) and in their own community (internal)' is taken from Gluck (1998: 34). The present

---

5. Here, the plural 'feminisms' is used to highlight the pluralism of women's movements, and to emphasize that women's collective action takes shape within many diverse times and places (see Bergman 2000: 153).

study delineates the development of feminist transformational action in Beijing since 1988. It began with (among other activities) one woman setting up a psychological counselling service and a small group of women setting up the Women's Research Institute; continued with the establishment and activities of several other organizations, groups and networks, such as the East Meets West Feminist Translation Group, the Beijing Sisters, the Centre for Women's Law Studies and Legal Services, the Women's Health Network and the Blue-stocking Group; and went on to the establishment of a national network against violence towards women.

Studies of women's organizing around the world recognize that engaging in the practice of organizing for change influences and alters activist perceptions of dominant gender relations and political power relations in society (Basu 1995, Chatty and Rabo 1997). Even though activists do not necessarily view themselves as political actors or articulate their organizing activities as political, women enter the political sphere of society through the act of organizing (Naples 1998: 329). Here, organizing is defined as political activity in the sense of being 'a method by which citizens and diverse groups and organizations, including corporations, attempt to create what they envision to be the good society' (Christensen-Ruffmann 1995: 374). In the process of organizing, the social reality addressed by activists is contrasted with the (gender) equality norms and discourse prevalent in their society. Furthermore, in practical organizational terms, organizing efforts are confronted with restrictions, especially in societies unaccustomed to organization from below. Thus, the process of organization within the context of diverse manifestations of (gender) equality discourse and social and political practice influences, develops and transforms participants' awareness of gender issues and political issues. This process of organizational practice has been the focus in studying the three Beijing organizations. Organization takes place within a conceptual and political space, and at the same time, it develops this space. Following the social movement theory of 'cognitive praxis' with its focus on the nature of social movements as producers of new knowledge and modes of action (Eyerman and Jamison 1991, 1998) and as producers of 'oppositional consciousness' (Sandoval 1991, Morris 1992), the process of organizing is viewed as a means of transforming and developing knowledge and practice related to gender, power and political participation. Organizing is a cultural and political process through which ideas and practices of gender and political participation are developed, renegotiated and reinterpreted, and the practice of gender and political participation is simultaneously changed. The 'cognitive praxis', in other words the process of creating and articulating new thoughts and ideas (new knowledge) and a collective identity, and the activism to which this leads, is the core activity of a social movement (Eyerman and Jamison 1991, 1998).

The Context of Women's Organizing in 1980s–1990s China

Throughout the world, historically and currently, women have acted and are acting collectively to create social change. Women's movements in different parts of the world embrace the diversity of women, the plurality of issues that they choose to address and their various modes of action. As recognized already nearly twenty years ago in a monumental volume on the global women's movement, 'its styles, strategies, and theoretical approaches are as varied as its composition is and its effects will be.' (Morgan 1984: 3). Despite local differences, transnational inspiration and influence and international cooperation are common features shared by women's movements. To mention just a few examples from the 1960–1980s movements: the women's movement in India in the 1970s was influenced by 'the women's liberation movement growing in the West with new ideas spreading' (Omvedt 1993: 80), and the Danish 'red-stocking movement' of the 1970–1980s was inspired by feminist action in the USA (Dahlerup 1998). The West German women's movement was influenced by movements in England, France, Italy and the German Democratic Republic (Altbach 1984: 458 cited in Margolis 1993: 385). Consciousness raising – one of the very central practices of the Euro-North American second-wave women's movements – was adopted from the revolutionary mode of 'speaking bitterness' found in the People's Republic of China (Ryan 1992: 167).[6] Furthermore, since the United Nations began to hold International Women's Conferences in 1975, movements in many parts of the world have been influenced by and drawn into the international women's movements by these conferences, their NGO Forums and not least the process of preparing for the conferences. Likewise, the present phase of women's organizing in China has been influenced by an exposure to international feminisms made possible by China's reforms and its 'opening' to the outside world. The 1995 United Nations Fourth World Conference

---

6. Erwin 2000: 165–166 gives an explanation of the historical origins and contemporary use of the practice of 'speaking bitterness'.

on Women, held in Beijing, played an important role in linking international feminisms and the women's movement in China (see Hsiung and Wong 1998, Wang Zheng 1997). Activists in China as well as women's studies academics have reached out to seek inspiration from women's movements in other parts of the world. This development has been facilitated by donor organizations and by feminist scholars from China who have studied and now work outside China, primarily in the USA, where they have established the Chinese Society for Women's Studies (CSWS). In 1993 the CSWS, in cooperation with the Centre for Women's Studies at Tianjin Normal University, held the first of several conferences in China aimed at facilitating exchange of feminist theory and practice. This conference has been defined as ground-breaking by and for Chinese activists.[7]

In the mid-1980s, when urban professional women began to organize on their own initiative in China, they broke away from the gender blindness of the Maoist period and reacted to the fact that the new phase of transformation of Chinese society, initiated in 1978, had a different influence on the lives of women than on those of men. Wang Zheng (1997: 127) notes: '[F]or many Chinese women who grew up in the People's Republic, especially urban women who were beneficiaries of equal educational and employment policies of the Maoist era, the CCP presumption that "Chinese women were liberated" was a fact beyond questioning.'[8] It is these urban academics and professional women who have set up the majority of organizing initiatives, including the three addressed in this volume, primarily for other women who are confronted with specific problems. The aim has been to address the specific, immediate needs of women who have been marginalized and subjugated in various ways, often as a consequence of economic reforms. These women are frequently in especially vulnerable positions as, for example, single mothers, laid-off workers or migrants. The aim has also been (at least for some forms of organizing), although at first perhaps not intentionally, to address the long-term and more fundamental changes needed to achieve gender equality and full citizenship. Various forms of organizing address the subordination of women, recognize gendered ex-

---

7. See Xiaolan Bao with Wu Xu 2001 for an overview of the first three CSWS workshops and the collaboration between scholars in China and the USA. For a critical appraisal of the transfer of Western feminist theory to China, see Spakowski 2001.

8. See also Lin Chun 1995b.

periences, provide social support and service, and work against abuse and for social justice and economic security. In short, these are activities that, implicitly or explicitly, claim full citizenship for women.

In the 1980s, a series of problems was specifically or disproportionately confronting women, political control was relatively relaxed, and academics began to travel to other countries. In this context, women's studies began to be established at universities.[9] Subsequently, various forms of women's groups, networks and organizations emerged and engaged in addressing issues of inequality and discrimination at a practical level. The three organizations covered here emerged in response to the negative impact of economic reform on the lives of women. Two particular problems that led to their establishment were a trend towards revival of traditional female submissive virtues and the growing disparity between official policy and rhetoric regarding gender equality and the inequalities seen and experienced in reality. These organizations, together with many others, are engaged in promoting the interests and welfare of women. They are doing so within a political context which now has begun to allow some degree of political activity outside of the direct initiative of party-state institutions. The party-state has also recognized to some degree that it is not able to cope with all social issues, and may thus need the contribution of private groups to address various problems in society.

Li Xiaojiang, director of the first academic women's studies centre[10] in reform period China has referred to the reaction of urban intellectual women to the negative consequences of reform as an awakening (*juexing*) of Chinese women's collective consciousness and a departure from an accustomed dependence on society in which gender equality was implemented from above by the party for women in

---

9. An *Interim Directory of Chinese Women's Organizations*, published by the Ford Foundation in Beijing in February 1995 for the Women's Conference, listed 15 university women's studies centres, all established since 1978. Eight were in the 3 municipalites of Beijing, Shanghai and Tianjin. A list published by the ACWF, also for the Women's Conference, included 5 'women's studies institutions of the Women's Federation system', 26 'academic institutions of women's studies', 21 'women's studies institutions in schools for higher learning' and 3 'women's studies institutions in the Academies of Social Sciences' (Quanguo fulian funü yanjiusuo 1995). See Du Fangqin 2001 for an overview of the development of women's studies.

10. See Jaschok 1998 for a study of 'the birth, life and closure of China's first institution of higher education with a women-centred programme.' The ACWF set up the Women's Studies Institute of China (Quanguo Fulian funü yanjiusuo) in 1991. Subsequently, similar centres were set up by provincial level Women's Federation branches.

terms of laws and regulations to protect women (Li Xiaojiang 1989). Implementation of laws and regulations was weakening and changes in attitude were taking place. For example, female college graduates were having trouble finding jobs because employers preferred their male fellow-graduates. Young women began to wonder whether they should concentrate on their own education and career, or, alternatively, find a husband and support him in his career. Developments like these led urban academics, such as Chen Yiyun, the director of the Jinglun Family Centre, to wonder:

> What a negative social phenomenon ... Why were women regressing after so many years of struggle and after having gained so much ... I just knew I could not bear to watch women taking this step backwards. (Chen Yiyun 1995: 34)

Furthermore, Li Xiaojiang has argued, the idea of women being inferior to men is deeply rooted in thousands of years of Chinese history. This meant that women regarded Communist Party legislation for gender equality as an immense favour. Women themselves would therefore have been the last to admit that despite attempts at creating change, inequality persisted (Li Xiaojiang 1991: 9–10).[11] A complementary interpretation is provided by Elisabeth Croll, who views women's silence in the PRC prior to the 1980s as the expression of a denial of women's experience. During the years of revolution (1949–78), a rhetoric of equality prescribed male and female equality and denied gender difference altogether. When there were discrepancies between this rhetoric and the actual experience of women, their experience was denied. There was simply no language with which to express actual experience when this experience did not match the rhetoric of equality, and one of the most marked characteristics of the reform period is the gradually more open recognition of the discrepancy between the rhetoric of equality and the female experience of inequality (Croll 1995). In the 1980s, changes in the political climate led to a more open academic debate and discussion of gender issues, and discrimination against women became so obvious that the silence was broken – primarily on behalf of other women – by the urban intellectual group, which itself had experienced a high degree of gender equality. Women embarked on a process of exploration of gender issues that has led to the intro-

---

11. For an in-depth study of Li Xiaojiang's early writings, see Frick, Leutner and Spakowski 1995.

duction of the concept of gender, and to heated debates on the meaning of feminism in the Chinese context (Min Dongchao 1998). The emerging market economy led to new opportunities as well as problems for both men and women. A series of issues developed specifically with regard to gender relations, the gender-based structuring of society and what was defined as 'an unequal competition between men and women' (Zhu Chuzhu 1990). These issues were increasingly debated in the media and led to an important discussion of alternative 'ways out for women' in the magazine *Women in China* (Naihua Zhang 1995: 25). The debate also came up in radio programmes (see e.g. Liang Jun 1989) and a book on 'ways out for women' by Li Xiaojiang (1989). Women experienced the following: disproportionate numbers of women workers were laid off by enterprises as they rationalized; young women had difficulty in entering universities and in gaining employment upon graduation; trafficking in women expanded; and girls in rural areas were denied access to education. All in all, the economic reforms revealed that structural changes since 1949, primarily in the form of women entering the paid labour force, had not really been accompanied by a fundamental change in gender relations after all. The family was still the basic unit of consumption and the primary unit responsible for caring for the weak, ill, or elderly, and, more importantly, its proper functioning was still primarily seen as women's responsibility. The reforms aggravated an already existing contradiction between structural change and a lack of change in gender relations and gave rise to a series of visible contradictions and conflicts specifically affecting the female population in both rural and urban China.[12] The 'Anti-Six Evils Campaign' (against trading in women, prostitution, gambling, drugs, feudal superstition and pornography) which was launched in 1989 by the government, and many similar campaigns since then, especially the 1992 'Law on the Protection of the Rights and Interests of Women', are indications that these problems began to be recognized officially. Simultaneously, urban women began organizing on their own initiative to take action and address these issues. Female infanticide and sex-specific abortions, both consequences of the limited number of births allowed per married couple under the 1979-initiated one-child family population policy combined with the preference for and eco-

---

12. For two early studies of the effects of the economic reforms on the lives of women, see Jacka 1990 and Tan Shen 1991. For a more recent overview, see Tan Lin and Peng Xizhe 2000.

nomic necessity of sons, were the most obvious indications of persistent gender inequality (see Johansson and Nygren 1991, Tu Ping 1993).

From the early 1980s, as the contradictory effects of economic reforms began to be felt, the political climate also allowed and encouraged academics to meet to discuss the problems created by the reform process (Bonnin and Chevrier 1991). Women began meeting in 'women's popular academic salons' (*funü minjian xueshu shalong*) (Liu Jinxiu 1991: 108), as they were called, to discuss the gender inequality which became vividly apparent in the reform period. Campus salons became a place where women who were worried about the implications of the contradictory effects of reform could gather, share grievances and begin to analyse the emerging situation. Guest speakers, discussion groups and small research projects characterized the early work of the women's salons. Many of their discussions centred around translations of Western feminist texts and books that began to appear in 1986 as part of the Collection on Women's Studies edited by the Zhengzhou University Women's Studies Research Centre.[13] This series represents a major scholarly effort to set modern Chinese women's studies in a theoretical framework. Salons also drew on the resources of visiting feminist scholars and the coveted materials that they brought with them. In Beijing salons were set up at Peking University – where women's studies were initiated in the early 1980s – and at the Beijing Foreign Languages Institute.

The move from discussion groups to action aimed at directing public attention towards gender inequality and creating political change was gradual. For example, the Women's Studies Forum at the Beijing Foreign Languages Institute was concerned about the fact that employers openly preferred male graduates applying for jobs to their female fellows. The first public activity of the Forum was a press conference held in 1989 on the problem of employment for women. The discussion group began to take on the characteristics of a social movement when it began to aim at creating broad change externally in the society as a whole instead of simply holding internal discussions for members. Off campus, one of the first women's organizations founded independently with the aim of influencing public opinion

---

13. One of the early translations of Western feminist texts, a volume edited by Duan Yongqiang (1987) was published by the ACWF publication house (Zhongguo funü chubanshe) as an internal publication (*neibu faxing*) not accessible to the public. The book included several texts translated by Li Xiaojiang, who was later to develop a somewhat controversial relationship to various levels of the Federation.

and policy making on gender issues was the Women's Research Institute (WRI), established in Beijing in October 1988 – the first of the organizations included in this book.

The relatively free rein given to women-focused activities throughout the 1980s and on into the 1990s may in part be explained by two things, one paradoxical, the other ironic. It is paradoxical that the party-state and women's organizations have a mutual interest with respect to implementation of the state population policy. Although strict limits on the number of children to which a woman may give birth and the practice of coerced abortion and contraceptive use constitute obvious repressions of women's self-determination (see Greenhalgh 1994, Milwertz 1997), the party-state and women's activists share an interest in eliminating those types of gender discrimination which stem from the preference for sons, such as female infanticide and violence against women who bear female children. These are very sensitive political issues which Chinese academics have only recently been able to address in publicly accessible forms, such as in the book *The Dual Effects of the Family Planning Program on Chinese Women* by Professor Zhu Chuzhu and her colleagues at Xi'an Jiaotong University (1997). It is ironic that the traditional legitimacy of women's liberation within communist ideology has meant that discussions on equal rights for women and men are generally viewed by the party-state as uncontroversial and politically unthreatening. They are imbued, in the words of three Chinese women's studies scholars, with 'ironic marginality' (Lin, Liu and Jin 1998: 109). The repeated broadcasting of a series of radio talks by sociologist Chen Yiyun on issues of marriage and family in June 1989, when regular radio-programmes had been suspended due to the Tiananmen Square demonstrations, illustrates their point. The programmes were instrumental in increasing Chen Yiyun's popularity. She had made the first attempts to set up an organization in 1988, and a few years after the 1989 broadcasts, she succeeded in setting up the Jinglun Family Centre – the second organization covered in this book. Although Chen Yiyun defines the Centre as a family rather than a women's organization and emphasizes that it is 'not a feminist organization', the centre is included here due to the role that it has played as part of the women's movement.

Beijing organizations, groups and networks

Women discovered that the relative political leeway that they had had during the 1980s was even more generous during 1993 and 1994, as China prepared to host the United Nations Fourth World

Conference on Women. Several groups, networks and organizations were established in Beijing during those years.[14] The following is a brief overview of some of these:

The East Meets West Feminist Translation Group was established in 1993 by a group of about ten bilingual women (both Chinese and non-Chinese). Their aim was to translate English-language texts from the second wave women's movements into Chinese in preparation for the Women's Conference. They could thus introduce the history and issues of those movements to a Chinese audience in order to bridge the cultural and terminological gaps created by the different social and political structures in China and the West.[15]

The Blue-stocking Group was set up by a group of academics engaged in editing a series of translations of women's literature published by the Institute for Foreign Literature at the Chinese Academy of Social Sciences in preparation for the Women's Conference. When work on the books was completed, the fourteen women editors decided to continue meeting. Their aim was to discuss personal and societal gender-related issues and women's literature. The group provided mutual support in personal and academic matters, and it organized meetings with guest speakers. These meetings were open to people outside the group and were covered by the media. The theme of one such meeting was 'Women, reform, progress', and the question posed was whether the reforms were bringing progress to women.

The Queer Women Group, later called the *Beijing Sisters*, was set up by a group of lesbians.[16] It did not, however, define itself as a formal group until 1998, although it began meeting informally in the early 1990s at small-scale private get-togethers. It aimed at sharing experiences of homosexuality in a non-condemning environment. When the group started organizing broader social movement activities, several of these were held in collaboration with homosexual men. In 1997, a Queer Pager Hotline offering advice to gays and lesbians was set up. In 1998 the First National Men and Women Queer Conference

---

14. See Wong Yuen Ling 1995 and Wang Yongchen 1995 for first-hand accounts of Chinese women's participation in the Women's Conference preparatory process. Other personal accounts of activism in organizations and women's studies are found in the following edited volumes: Liu Guanghua 1999, Li Xiaojiang 2000, and Hsiung, Jaschok and Milwertz 2001. See also Du Fangqin 1997.

15. See Ge and Jolly 2001 for an account of the establishment and development of the East Meets West Feminist Translation Group.

16. See He Xiaopei 2001 for an account of the establishment of the Queer Women Group/Beijing Sisters.

was held in Beijing. Thirty homosexual women and men from several provinces as well as from Hong Kong, Taiwan and foreign countries attended. In the autumn of 1998, the First National Queer Women Conference was held in Beijing, and since 1999 a lesbian magazine – *Sky (Tiankong)* has been published.[17]

The Association for Promoting Rural Women in Development was established in 1993 under the leadership of Luo Xiaolu, a journalist and vice-president of the Beijing Women's Federation. The organization grew out of the rural women's section of the Beijing Women's Theoretical Research Society and a two-day seminar on rural women and development that was held in 1993. The aim of the Association was to link urban and rural women in order to develop rural women's technical and agricultural skills and to influence policymaking by focusing attention on issues related to rural women and development.

The Women's Health Network was established in September 1993 by a group of fifteen women. The Network was primarily set up for the exchange of information about ongoing organization activities, as members were already engaged in these. The main activity, which started prior to the Women's Conference and was completed in 1998, was the translation and publication of the book put out by the Boston Women's Health Collective, *Our Bodies, Ourselves*, into Chinese. The book had been introduced at the 1993 seminar held by the Women's Studies Centre at Tianjin Normal University and the Chinese Society for Women's Studies. A few Network members thought the book unsuitable for China due to its critical feminist outlook. Others thought that they could use the spirit, perspective and principles of the book as a basis from which to write a Chinese version. As a result, the decision was made first to translate and publish the book in Chinese and later to write two Chinese books – one for women and one for men.

The China–Canada Young Women's Project was started by two students – Liu Dongxiao from China and Kimberley Manning from Canada – in order to make young women's voices heard at the Women's Conference. They wanted to strengthen cooperation between different generations of women, and by asking established women's organiza-

---

17. In April 2001 the Chinese Psychiatric Association declared that homosexuality was no longer defined as a disease. However, when lesbian artists attempted to hold a public meeting on 1 May, they were prevented from doing so by Public Security. Whether this was due to the lesbian theme of their meeting , the politically sensitive timing, or both, is unclear.

tions to accept young women as volunteers, they wanted the older women to pass their experience on to younger women. Members of the group participated in translating *Our Bodies, Ourselves*, they acted as translators for the Women's Research Institute and they published a newsletter during preparations for the Women's Conference. The group gave young women a chance to exchange experiences and reflect on the structural rather than personal nature of many of their problems. They passed on their new knowledge to other young women via the newsletter, and defined the chance to engage in this learning process as more important to them than the Conference itself.[18]

In 1993 a Legal Advice Service was established by the Women's Health Network and Pi Xiaoming, a lawyer employed by one of Beijing's city district Women's Federations – the East District Women's Federation. In 1995 another legal aid service centre – the Centre for Women's Law Studies and Legal Services (CWLSLS) – was established. The CWLSLS is engaged in researching the legal system as it concerns women. Both organizations provide legal advice to individuals through face-to face counseling and telephone hotlines, and they provide free legal services. They publish articles in newspapers and produce radio programs in order to create an awareness of legal issues and increase the legal literacy of the population in general. An important overall aim is to influence policymakers to improve laws and the legal system as such.

Outside China, the best-known Beijing organizations are those which have received donor funding from Europe and North America. This applies to most of the organizations mentioned above. Donor funding has made activities possible when no other funding was available. Their receipt of donor funding and engagement in feminist ideologies and practices have also led to the criticism that these organizing activities are not truly Chinese but that they have been planted and nurtured by outsiders. In China, as in other Third World countries, feminists who challenge historically dominant patriarchal ideologies and practices in their countries are routinely (as discussed in relation to women in India by Uma Narayan 1997) accused of adopting a Western ideology that is incompatible with their home cultures. As this volume will demonstrate, although influenced by transnational and cross-cultural interaction, grassroots initiated activism

---

18. See Milwertz 1996 for an interview with Liu Dongxiao on the China–Canada Young Women's Project.

in Beijing is firmly rooted in issues pertaining to particular local political, social, economic and cultural contexts. Similarly, the modes of action that women have chosen to apply in order to address these issues are rooted in the context of the political culture of their work.

During the years leading up to the Women's Conference, another type of women's organization – for professional women – was also being established. Examples are the national-level Chinese Women Mayors' Association, established in 1991 on the initiative of a woman vice-mayor from Nanning, Guangxi, and provincial and municipal level organizations, such as the Capital Women Journalists' Association, set up in Beijing in 1986. Membership in both, as in most professional organizations, is automatic by virtue of employment in the professional sphere.

The All China Women's Federation

The new organizations rode the wave broken by Chinese authorities, who were eager to rehabilitate an international reputation which had been badly damaged in 1989, and confident of their comparative achievements in the area of women's rights. These achievements are very much the merit of the All China Women's Federation: it is impossible to address women's activities of organizing from below without relating these activities to the Federation.[19]

The Federation was set up by the Communist Party with the dual objective of communicating Party policy downwards through the administrative system to women and of representing women by transmitting grassroots opinions upwards.[20] Coinciding with political rollercoaster developments in China, the Federation was revived in the reform period, after having been closed down during the Cultural Revolution. The federation is, as its name implies, a conglomeration of several organizations. In April 1997 the ACWF had nineteen national-level group members (*tuanti huiyuan*) (ACWF officials, inter-

---

19. At the 1999 workshop 'Women Organizing in China' at the University of Oxford, Liu Guanghua, initiator and director of the Huaguang Women's College, a popular women's organization in Nanning, Guangxi, objected to the way in which new forms of organizing are routinely defined in relation to the ACWF, thereby privileging the ACWF. While the objection is relevant, the ACWF is also unquestionably the largest women's organization in China, and it is impossible to understand new, small organizations without relating them to the ACWF.

20. Naihua Zhang 2001 provides a fascinating overview of the dual role of the Women's Federation.

view 27 March 1997).[21] The majority of these are professional organizations for women lawyers, mayors, journalists and so on. The Women's Research Institute was also a member for some years. Membership implies that these organizations operate under the leadership of the ACWF.

Despite the establishment of other organizations within recent years, the Federation is indisputably the main organizer and representative of women in China. Federation policy and attitudes towards organizing from below outside of its domain have been complex, ranging from cooperation to conflict. Since its revival, the Federation has made attempts to transfer its main loyalties from the party to its constituency, to reform its methods and to become more autonomous. In this context, it is extremely sensitive to the challenge to its near-exclusive position as the representative of Chinese women's interests (White, Howell and Shang 1996, Howell 1997b; see also Wang Zheng 1997 on the changing role of the ACWF). Although the organization constitutes an extensive multi-level system reaching out to all parts of the country, the mere size and outreach of the ACWF has apparently not been sufficient for the national level organization to feel secure in its position and able to cooperate magnanimously with new initiatives set up outside its purview. In 1988, when its role as more or less exclusive representative of women began to be challenged, the ACWF included a total of 98,589 cadres (party functionaries) working at 68,355 branches at all administrative levels of the country from the provinces to rural villages and urban street committees (Zhonghua quanguo ... 1991: 576–577). By comparison, the new organizations – including the three covered in this volume – are minute in terms of number of staff, members and volunteers. The Women's Hotline run by the Women's Research Institute/Maple Women's Psychological Counselling Centre, which is the women's organizing activity in Beijing engaging the largest number of activists, includes about 50 volunteer counsellors, each working one or two afternoons or evenings per month at the telephone. The threat is not in numbers, but rather that the ACWF has still to come to terms with its new status as one of many voices representing women. The Migrant Women's Club – the third organization included in this book – was established within the framework of the ACWF. Established after the Women's

---

21. According to the ACWF website www.women.org.cn (updated in April 2000), 'there are 18 national group members and about 5,800 local group members at various levels throughout the country'.

Conference, it was set up in recognition of the general problems pertaining to the gap between urban and rural populations and gender-specific problems encountered by female rural migrants in the urban context.

Popular organizing

Various terms, including non-governmental organization (NGO), 'grass-roots' and 'popular', have been applied to define the new types of self-initiated, bottom-up organizing that have emerged or re-emerged in the 1980s and 1990s in China. Before the concept of the non-governmental organization was introduced to China, the term generally used to designate this type of organizing was 'popular' (*minjian*). For example, in an article published in 1991, Liu Jinxiu defined two types of 'women's popular organizations' (*funü minjian zuzhi*), which developed in the 1980s (Liu Jinxiu 1991).[22]

In connection with preparations for the United Nations Fourth World Conference on Women, the concept of NGO was introduced to women's organizing in China. All three organizations included in this study define themselves as NGOs. They use either the English language term, the direct Chinese translation *feizhengfu zuzhi,* or the English-Chinese combinations *NGO-zuzhi* [NGO-organization] or *minjian-NGO* [popular NGO] to distinguish the new forms of organizing from the organizations and institutions established and led by the party-state.[23]

To define themselves as NGOs is problematic, because in 1994 '[t]o counteract the rejection and claim the ACWF's legitimacy in its involvement in the organization of the Beijing NGO Forum, the Chinese government formally termed the ACWF "China's largest NGO that aims at raising the status of women" in the *Report of the People's Republic of China on the Implementation of the Nairobi Forward-Looking Strategies for the Advancement of Women*' (Naihua Zhang 2001). Although the ACWF carries out many functions similar to those of women's NGOs in other countries, it did not become an NGO by being defined as such, primarily because the organization is character-ized by its dual role as transmitter of party-state policy and as a

---

22. These were the professional women's organizations which are group members of the ACWF, and those initiatives that were set up by intellectual women without direct dependency on party-state institutions.
23. In a recent publication, Wang Xingjuan (2000) defines the Women's Research Institute/Maple Women's Psychological Counselling Centre as a grassroots organization (*caogen zuzhi*); however, this term is seldom used.

representative of women. It is an organization established by the party-state, and one of its main functions is to convey party-state policy to its constituency – i.e. all women in China. Because it plays this latter role, it would have been counterproductive to addressing issues of gender inequality in Chinese society if the ACWF had been excluded from non-governmental preparations for the 1995 Women's Conference NGO Forum and the Forum itself, and as such, international acceptance of the sudden NGO status made sense.

The ACWF has the characteristics of both a governmental and a non-governmental organization, and is often defined in China as a 'semi-official/semi-popular' (*banguan banmin*) organization. Naihua Zhang (2001) has argued for the recognition of the ACWF as an NGO as a matter of international recognition of Chinese women's agency in the specific Chinese political context. In general on the domestic level, activists in popular organizing either do not recognize the ACWF as an NGO or they distinguish between various types of NGOs. Sociologist Chen Yiyun, who is also director of the Jinglun Family Centre, defines three types of NGOs: first, party-state initiated organizations such as the ACWF and the Women Workers' Department of the Trade Union; second, academic women's studies institutes; and third, what she calls 'pure' or 'real' NGOs. This third category includes organizations such as the Jinglun Family Centre, the Women's Research Institute and the Women's Health Network.[24]

The definition of various organizations as governmental or non-governmental is further complicated by formal registration requirements. Whereas the Women's Research Institute/Maple Women's Psychological Counselling Centre and the Jinglun Family Centre are structurally independent of the ACWF, the Migrant Women's Club was set up as part of the All China Women's Federation. If the ACWF is defined as a government organization, can the Migrant Women's Club then be an NGO set up within a government organization? Or should the ACWF be recognized as an NGO? Although these are intriguing and important questions, they are not addressed in this volume. Here, all types of organizing initiated from below by the activists themselves, regardless of whether they are institutionally affiliated to, registered with or set up within an established party-state organization or not, are defined as *popular*, in the sense of a political

---

24. See also Li Xiaojiang 1997 for a discussion of 'Who are China's women's NGOs?'. For a discussion of the problematic concept of NGOs in China, see Sausmikat 2001.

activity 'of or carried on by the people as a whole rather than restricted to politicians or political parties' (Pearsall 1998: 1443). They are so defined, even though the activities are carried out not by 'the people as a whole' but by relatively small groups of citizens.[25] The term NGO is used only when activists themselves use the term. Generally, they use the term 'NGO' to convey 'bottom-up' activity and a spirit of activism and independent action rather than structural aspects of organizing.

Methodological notes

Three organizations – the Women's Research Institute/Maple Women's Psychological Counselling Centre, Jinglun Family Centre and Migrant Women's Club, established in Beijing in 1988, 1993 and 1996 respectively – form the core of this study.

The main data consists of a series of qualitative interviews with the initiators of these organizations. The three organizations differ both in terms of their activities and in terms of the types of activists who are involved in the activities. Due to these differences, as well as to the different set-ups of the three organizations and the varying degrees of accessibility to people engaged in them, interviews were carried out with different groups of people in each organization. These differences are reflected in the way in which each of the three organizations is presented in the following chapters.

Chapter Two, on the Women's Research Institute (WRI), is based on interviews with Director Wang Xingjuan, with two other initiators of the Institute, and with nine Hotline counsellors, of whom four have been counsellors since the Women's Hotline started in 1992, and of whom three are Hotline supervisors. Although only a few names appear in the text, the chapter is based on all these interviews as well as on written materials about the Institute and the Centre.[26]

Chapter Three, on the Jinglun Family Centre (JFC), describes the establishment and development of the Centre in the form of a one-person narrative. Because the interviews span several years (1994 to 1998), both optimistic and pessimistic moments in the history of the

---

25. Jaschok (1998: 324) defines *minjian* as 'independent grassroots', while Cornue (1999: 89) characterizes the term as 'people-to-people'. The term 'popular' is not used here in the sense of being liked, admired, or enjoyed by many people. When reading a draft of this book, the director of one of the three organizations expressed concern that the use of the term 'popular' might be understood by the ACWF and the authorities to convey this particular meaning, and that it was therefore politically unwise to use the term.

organizations are reflected in the chapters, perhaps especially in the one on the JFC. The narrative conveys a process of organizational ups and downs which illustrate how organizing for social change can be an exhilarating experience of successful achievement, but also how it can simply be exhaustingly hard and lonely work for those who are the driving force behind such activities. This is especially the case when the political climate becomes tense, as it did in 1995–96, when the WRI was in an extremely sensitive political situation. During the following year, when I had planned to meet JFC activists, the political climate surrounding the Jinglun Family Centre was tense, visits by foreigners were being registered, and phone calls were quite possibly being monitored. A main reason for the choice of the narrative form in the chapter on the Jinglun Family Centre is that most of my interviews were with Chen Yiyun. Although many activists were engaged in the work of the Centre, they were not physically present at the Centre offices on a daily basis. They wrote for the Centre and they gave talks and lectures, but my impression was that they did not regularly come into the office. Despite the fact that I often visited the Centre office during stays in Beijing, I did not meet these activists.

Because the Women's Hotline is based at the WRI, visits to the Institute led to meetings with Hotline counsellors. I was also invited to take part in several activities, such as, for example, the Women's Conference reception and NGO Forum workshop and a 1997 Maple Women's Psychological Counselling Centre two-day training course for Hotline volunteer counsellors. Whereas participation in these activities led to subsequent meetings and interviews with WRI/MWPCC activists, similar opportunities did not arise at the Jinglun Family Centre.

Interviews for Chapter Four on the Migrant Women's Club include interviews with five main activists and staff of the Club (primarily the two Club initiators – Director Xie Lihua and advisor and co-initiator Professor Wu Qing) and with eight Club members. These interviews were supplemented with observations made at organized Club activities and during a series of visits to the Club.

---

26. In connection with major anniversaries and other events, the Women's Research Institute and Maple Women's Psychological Counselling Center have published detailed accounts of their activities. See Hongfeng 1998, Zhongguo guanli 1994a, Zhongguo guanli 1995a. These brochures provide rich information on the establishment, history and development of the two organizations as well as a 'Chronology of Important Events 1988–98' (Hongfeng 1998: 14–29).

Data collection and analysis have been guided by an inductive grounded theory approach. The first interviews with leaders of two of the organizations – Chen Yiyun, director of the Jinglun Family Centre and Wang Xingjuan, director of the Women's Research Institute – took place in October 1994. In a way, the research project grew out of those interviews, which were conducted as part of the collection of data for the book *Fra Maosko til Laksko* [From cloth shoes to patent leather] on women in China's reform period, which I co-authored with Qi Wang, a political scientist at Aarhus University (Milwertz and Wang 1995). The book was published in Denmark by the women's organization KULU – Women and Development (Kvindernes U-landsudvalg) – in preparation for the 1995 United Nations Fourth World Conference on Women. Subsequently, interviews with Chen Yiyun and Wang Xingjuan as well as with Xie Lihua and Wu Qing, and with activists, took place over the course of six visits to China in 1996, 1997 and 1998, adding up to a total of six months spent there. The source material includes newspaper and magazine articles about the three organizations and articles written by activists from the organizations; reports written by leaders of the organizations following participation at meetings; and bulletins, brochures and reports on the organizations' work, published by the organizations themselves.

As will be seen, the three chapters on each of the organizations are different in form. All include passages from the interviews and Chapter Three on the Jinglun Family Centre (JFC) is constructed as one long narrative. The directors of The Women's Research Institute and the Jinglun Family Centre each read and commented on draft versions of the chapter covering their organization. Xie Lihua has read an earlier version of the chapter on the Migrant Women's Club, which was translated into Chinese, and the current English version was sent to Wu Qing. Some changes have been made subsequently; however, I bear full responsibility for the final text.

2

The Women's Research Institute and Maple Women's Psychological Counselling Centre

In 1988 when journalist and editor Wang Xingjuan retired, she wanted to do something for women. For some years she had been investigating the problems which confronted women as a result of the economic reforms, and upon realizing that very few were engaged in this research, she wanted to gather people who were concerned about these issues. She invited about twenty people to meet in her home and discuss what they could do together. The result was that in October 1988, after several meetings and many discussions, the Women's Research Institute (WRI), the predecessor to the Maple Women's Psychological Counselling Centre (MWPCC), was set up in Beijing. In her speech at the inaugural meeting Wang Xingjuan, who became the director of the Institute, described its main aim as follows:

> China's opening to the rest of the world, the reconstruction of the market economy, and intense social competition have all begun to challenge women's gains in status and rights. We have no choice but to recognize the fact that those of our sisters who are independent enough to adapt successfully to the overwhelming challenges in the competitive market economy are only a fraction of those struggling to survive. Reality tells us that achieving women's complete liberation is still a challenging and arduous task. Therefore, what the WRI strives for is to help women recognize their own rights, solve their problems, develop their own abilities, and not only adapt to but also succeed in the rapidly developing society. In summary, initiating women's own awakening is the demand of our time; it is also the principle of the Women's Research Institute. (Women's Research Institute 1995: 2).

In 1994 Wang Xingjuan proudly defined the WRI as '[t]he first women's research institute in China. Even the All China Women's Federation women's studies centre was established later. And even though Li Xiaojiang's Centre[1] was established a year earlier, it was a centre, not a research institute'. Similarly to the women's studies centres that were beginning to be established in the late 1980s at universities, the WRI was set up by a group of activists on their own initiative. While this in itself was exceptional in the China of the 1980s, an additional exceptional feature of the WRI was that it was not set up within or affiliated to a university, the Women's Federation or any other party-state institution. The WRI was set up 'in order to provide help to women based on the strength of society, for women themselves to help women and not to be completely dependent on the government' (Wang Xingjuan, interview, 11 October 1994). The history of the WRI, including its transformation into and continued struggle as the MWPCC, is closely linked to the innovation in PRC society of organizing planned and effectuated from below on the initiative of activists themselves. From the very beginning, the strengths as well as the weaknesses of the Institute have been linked to its status as a popular organization. This has influenced practically all aspects of the Institute, from the content of its activities and the structure of the organization to its growth and very survival.

Applied research

Initially, as the name indicates, the main aim of the Women's Research Institute was to provide support to women by researching some of the many problems that they encountered in relation to the economic reforms. The group that Wang Xingjuan originally invited to meet in her home included, among others, Professor Jin Nan from the Chinese Institute of Personnel and Human Resources Science and editor Xie Lihua from the newspaper *China Women's News* – two women who had actively engaged in research and debate on some of the many issues confronting women.[2] Based on her research, Jin Nan had proposed the establishment of a central fund to cover expenses incurred by enterprises in connection with maternity leave, since

---

1. The Women's Studies Research Centre at Zhengzhou University (Zhengzhou daxue funüxue yanjiu zhongxin).
2. Jin Nan's main argument was that the time women spend bringing up children is a contribution towards society, and that society at large, rather than the individual enterprise, should bear the economic responsibility of maternity leave.

Figure 1: Wang Xingjuan with two co-initiators of the Women's Research Institute – Professor Jin Nan of the Chinese Institute of Personnel and Human Resources Science and Xie Lihua, editor, *China Women's News*. (Photo: The Women's Research Institute)

state-funded maternity leave had been withdrawn in connection with privatization, thus causing discrimination against women in the labour force. Xie Lihua had organized several important discussions in *China Women's News* on problems confronting women.[3] According to Wang Xingjuan, the WRI aimed to go beyond historical research and 'empty theory' to provide research that would help to solve specific and concrete issues confronting women. This form of applied research was primarily viewed as the responsibility of the government and party-state institutions. Nonetheless, WRI activists wanted to contribute, especially with research on topics which they felt were not being given appropriate attention by academic institutions or the Women's Federation. In 1996, not long before the WRI became the MWPCC, Wang Xingjuan defined the eight years of WRI research as follows:

> The Women's Federation has done a lot of research. However, we have researched topics that they don't study, such as for example employment issues. They have carried out a nationwide study of women's position, but it does not include employment issues in the

3. Jin Nan and Xie Lihua became the first deputy directors of the Institute.

same way as our work. And look at women's political participation – they feel this issue is too – well, they don't seem to want to investigate this topic. We looked at the falling rates of women's political participation. Why were they decreasing? Was there a social cause or was this a problem related to women themselves? We felt that such questions had to be researched. Another issue is prostitution – they do not do studies on prostitution either. This is a sensitive issue. But prostitutes are a social group now. And the phenomenon has an impact on society. But if you don't engage in research, then how can you propose countermeasures and how can you solve problems? Our studies are concerned with very new and contemporary women's issues. And we don't do research for its own sake. We don't think that once we have published our work, our task is completed. We aim to make a contribution to society. We want the leadership to listen to our recommendations and suggestions. We emphasize how our findings can help women. How research findings can aid understandings of women's position and difficulties – how women can find solutions to problems confronting them. (Wang Xingjuan, interview 1996)

The first WRI research project was concerned with employment issues, specifically with the fact that the majority of laid-off workers during the reform period were women.[4] Prostitution, which re-emerged in Chinese society in the 1980s, was another early research topic. In April 1988 the WRI, in cooperation with the Social Survey Institute of the China Academy of Management Science, held a national seminar on 'Prostitution, use of prostitutes and countermeasures' (Maiyin piaochang ji duice yantaohui). According to the WRI, this was the first time in China that academics from the social sciences and other disciplines and practitioners from public security and the judiciary began to address this sensitive issue (Hongfeng 1998:5). As the Institute lacked funding to carry out research, collection of data for a third research topic was linked to a series of management training courses for women cadres, which the Institute held in order to raise funds for research activities. Nine training courses were held, with between forty and fifty participants attending each. All participants were asked to fill in a questionnaire, which then provided the main set of data for a study of women's political participation. This manner of linking research to other activities soon became a characteristic feature of WRI work.

---

4. The research report 'Trends in the employment of women in China' (Zhongguo shehui funü jiuye qushi yanjiu) was published in the ACWF magazine *Woman Work* (Funü gongzuo). See Zhongguo guanli 1990a, 1990b.

The Hotlines – combining practical social support and research

In May 1991 the WRI set up its first non-research activity – the Singles' Weekend Club (Danshen zhoumo julebu). In September 1992 the first Women's Hotline (Funü rexian) was started. Volunteer counsellors included both WRI activists and newly recruited counsellors. They were mainly academics and teachers, and there were quite a few journalists. The Club and the Women's Hotline were set up in order to offer practical support and because they provided a means of securing funding for WRI activities. Club members paid a membership fee and establishment of the Hotline was based on a grant from a non-Chinese donor organization – the Global Fund for Women. Finally, these activities offered a rich source of data for future research. Since then, research activities have been linked to or have grown out of these practical activities. Based on calls to the Hotline, activist researchers became aware of social problems such as domestic violence, sexual harassment and incest. The problems became visible, and data was systematically collected to document their nature and extent. In addition to the first Women's Hotline and the Singles' Weekend Club, practical social support provided by the WRI/MWPCC has included reproductive health education for migrant women, training of women cadres and Hotline counsellors, the Ark Family Centre (Fangzhou jiating zhongxin) and a rural poverty alleviation project. Two additional hotlines were established in the early 1990s – the Women's Expert Hotline (Funü zhuanjia rexian),[5] and the second Women's Hotline.[6] They were established as a core function of the WRI and were later developed by the MWPCC.[7] In 1998 the

---

5. The Women's Expert Hotline provides services on legal matters, marriage and family issues, maternal and child care, and sex.
6. Several WRI/MWPCC publications describe and analyse how Women's Hotline skills and knowledge of psychological counselling have developed, see Wang and Wang (eds) 2000 and Yang Mei 1997b.
7. During the first 256 days of the Hotline, 3,618 calls were received (Zhongguo guanli 1994a). For statistics on Hotline callers and the reasons they contacted the Hotline in the first year, see Zhongguo guanli 1994a. For the period from 1992 to 1997, see Hongfeng 1998: 38–40. The Hotlines are national. When the first Hotline opened, 60 per cent of calls came from Beijing. In 1995 the ratio between Beijing and the rest of the country was 54:46. Very few calls are made from rural areas and 80 per cent of calls come from big and medium sized cities (Yang Mei 1997a). Development of the Hotlines is linked to the expansion of telephone usage in China. For statistics on the development of and access to telephone technology in China, see Cornue 1999: 76–77. For a study of the implications of the emergence of telephone hotlines in China in terms of a transformation of the nature of personal matters and private concerns from private to public, see Erwin 2000.

Figure 2: The Women's Hotline in 1994. (Photo: Kirstine Theilgaard)

Aging Women's Hotline (Laonian funü rexian) was started. Most calls are from Beijing, but calls do come in from the whole country. The Hotline objective, which emphasises the link between research and social support, is reflected in the slogan: 'women studying women, women supporting women, women educating women' (*nüxing yanjiu nüxing, nüxing bangzhu nüxing, nüxing jiaoyu nüxing*). Research is the basis for providing Hotline support, knowledge and information to callers, and at the same time, the Hotlines provide data for further research.

ℰↄ Domestic violence research

Several studies on the prevalence of domestic violence in China had been carried out when the WRI became aware of and began to study the issue. In 1994 Wang Xingjuan explained:

> We started the Hotline, and there were often calls from women who had been beaten by their husbands. Some women attempt suicide. They feel that when their marriage is over, their life is over too. We have had calls from more than one woman who tells us that her husband brings his mistress to their home and then requires the wife to serve them both. Especially those who are beaten severely are in trouble. We have no shelter for battered women. There is nothing we can do. We can only tell them to go to whatever work-unit they

belong to or to contact the Women's Federation legal advisory unit, the Trade Union or the local street committee. Or to go to the courts and prosecute if they have been beaten severely.

Question: Why do these women call the Hotline? Is there nowhere else to go?

No. If they tell others, they (the 'others') are often unwilling to provide support. In 1991 the ACWF national study had shown that 0.4 per cent of women were being beaten by their husbands. This figure is very, very low. Then the Population Research Institute at the Chinese Academy of Social Sciences published a study which said that 1.67 per cent of urban women were being beaten by their husband. The rural rate was 4.68 per cent. According to a Beijing study 21 per cent of women were being beaten. Our impression from the Hotline calls was that this was a serious problem. So we carried out a study of thirty urban cases. We wanted to know which people beat their wives in urban China, and we found that violence also takes place in the homes of intellectuals. Some men who are university professors, journalists, or company directors – they also beat their wives. Now we are analysing one hundred Hotline cases. In the past we thought that women being beaten was not a problem; now we realize that there is a problem. It is impossible to compare with pre-reform period conditions, as there were no studies, no statistics. In the past, no one took any notice of this type of violence. The Hotline has made the problem visible. (Wang Xingjuan, interview 1994).[8]

℘ Sexual harassment research

Early WRI research[9] also included a study on sexual harassment undertaken by Hotline counsellor and supervisor Le Ping (1995a, 1995b), who explains:

Often these cases involved women who were being harassed by their bosses at work, and they were afraid of losing their jobs if they protested. There was nowhere to make a complaint. So we decided to investigate in order to determine exactly what the problems were and what could be done. How should China legislate in order to protect women's rights? And how could the problem be made known in society in order to change public opinion? Generally, people don't have adequate knowledge of sexual harassment. They think that it is a women's issue rather than a men's issue and a moral issue

---

8. See Wang Xingjuan n.d. and 1995b for results of domestic violence studies.
9. Sociologist Tang Can was one of the first scholars to write about the issue of sexual harassment – see Tang Can 1996.

rather than a rights issue. Women become extremely anxious and many work units will not do anything. Before the reforms this type of problem was resolved administratively and disciplinary action was taken. Now nobody seems to bother to do anything. Some leaders find this kind of problem difficult to resolve, so the psychological pressure on the victims is very big. We console them and teach them how to cope with the situation. We tell women to show the violator that they definitely do not approve of his actions. We provide methods of coping to the individual woman who encounters sexual harassment. First of all, we tell callers that their rights have been violated and that they must protect their rights. Many people do not know that their rights have been violated. Most view sexual harassment as a very terrible behaviour. In China we call this hooligan behaviour (*liumang xingwei*), or immoral behaviour.

In general, we need to educate the public. Many people don't realize what sexual harassment is. The concept of sexual harassment came to China from the USA because there was a case about an American woman engaged in a lawsuit which was publicized in China. Many women do not know that the behaviour they encounter is sexual harassment. The phenomenon exists but it has been viewed only as a question of immorality. It has only been evaluated from a moral perspective as something that ought not to take place. But it has not been viewed from a legal perspective or a rights perspective. I want to propose that China should legislate on this issue and that work units should have regulations on sexual harassment to protect women. There should also be public education so that people understand what sexual harassment is and that it is a violation of women's rights. And women should be aware of how to handle sexual harassment. Men will have to be careful, they will have to restrain themselves. Many people don't understand. The common attitude is that if a woman encounters sexual harassment, it is because she is not being proper, because something is wrong with the way she dresses or the way she acts. To my mind this is not equality. This is a not a correct understanding of sexual harassment. Instead it should be viewed as a social issue. The Hotline can help women who encounter problems and we can analyse cases so that we can improve our understanding of problems and help even more callers. (Le Ping, interviews 1994, 1996)

✤ Changing perceptions – women's awareness, gender awareness and empowerment

In 1995 the WRI held the workshop 'Women's Groups and Social Support' (*Funü qunti yu shehui jiuzhu*) at the United Nations Women's

Figure 3: The 1995 NGO Forum workshop 'Women's Groups and Social Support'. (Photo: Cecilia Milwertz)

Conference NGO Forum in Beijing. The NGO Forum workshop was remarkable and significant both because WRI activists addressed politically sensitive and socially taboo issues, and because it was the only workshop held by one of the new popular women's organizations in China. Activists from several of these organizations took part in the NGO Forum and some presented papers at a number of the many Chinese workshops. However, the WRI was the only popular women's organization to hold an independent workshop. The workshop presented results of WRI research and Hotline counselling on domestic violence, sexual harassment and prostitution, among other topics, thus documenting Hotline experience and research results, focusing on politically sensitive issues and emphasizing the importance of recognizing these. This was not an easy feat, as this comment by a WRI activist illustrates:

> When we applied for participation at the Women's Conference NGO Forum, the theme of our workshop included domestic violence and sexual harassment. The All China Women's Federation was worried about these topics [laughs]. However, in the end our topics were accepted, but the ACWF was scared. For example, if the ACWF says there is no domestic violence in China and you say there is a lot, this can be rather problematic, if you see what I mean. (WRI activist, interview 1996)

However, the fact that the China Women Judges' Association held a workshop on violence against women illustrated that the ACWF ended up deciding that it would be possible to discuss the issue at the NGO Forum. Understandings of the issue of domestic violence have varied, as have attitudes towards it, not only among women's organizations, but also internally within the WRI among Hotline counsellors. Some counsellors are convinced that a victim of domestic violence categorically should not accept violence and should, for example, leave her husband, whereas others believe that the primary duty of a woman – as a wife and a mother – is to mediate and to maintain family harmony by remaining in a relationship despite violence. Wang Xingjuan explains that official Hotline attitudes have changed over the years:

> ... we require that counsellors must have women's awareness (*funü yishi*) in their work.[10] This means that their work must be based on a women's standpoint. They must defend women's rights. They must help women to improve their self-confidence. Our counselling perspective cannot be based on the ideology of traditional society. The traditional ideology takes the view that in the case of domestic violence the woman is too fierce; she is always jabbering away, and finally the husband becomes anxious and impatient and has no other option than to hit her. In other words, it is the woman's own fault if her husband beats her. We do not agree with this. Regardless of how much a woman talks, it is wrong for a man to hit her. This is women's awareness.

> *Question: At the training session for new Hotline volunteers recently* [summer 1998] *you said that you attended a meeting in India earlier this year, which influenced you very much. Could you explain a bit about that?*

> This was a meeting on domestic violence – the women's awareness of the people there influenced me deeply. It was very educational. They made a clear distinction and said that psychological counselling – including face-to-face counselling and hot line counselling – must be distinguished by whether they are based on women's awareness or not. They gave many examples like the one I just mentioned. For example, does the counsellor say to the caller, who is a victim of

---

10. The term *funü yishi* is used in the sense of 'women's subjective awareness' or 'women's self-consciousness' referring to women's regaining of a gender identity in terms of realization rather than denial of their difference as members of the female sex, a difference that was erased by equality politics in the Mao era. I thank Qi Wang for discussions concerning this and many other terms.

domestic violence: 'You should talk less. If your husband does not like you to talk so much, then you should talk less, and he will not beat you.' This would be the response based on traditional ideology. Based on women's awareness, men and women are equal and it is not right for men to hit women. First and foremost, we have to point out to the caller that she has not done anything wrong, and that it is wrong for her husband to hit her. At the meeting in India they pointed out that these two responses to a caller are fundamentally different and that we should not only provide counselling but also education in women's awareness. *Aiya* – when I heard this I realized that we had not previously included this in our training of counsellors. So at the training session for new counsellors that day we emphatically stressed the importance of applying women's awareness in our Hotline counselling.

This year during a meeting in Hong Kong we realised that women scholars in Hong Kong have a much stronger feminist position than we do.[11] For example we discussed a chapter on extramarital relationships. We had written that the wife should constrain herself and exercise patience. The whole chapter was about how the wife should endure and put up with her husband's behaviour. Our colleagues in Hong Kong thought that our attitude was not feminist (*nüxing zhuyi*). Our position had been that however many relationships a husband had, the woman could only endure. They said that this was not empowering. They thought that our attitude was incorrect and that we should look at the problem from an empowerment perspective. We agreed and subsequently revised the whole chapter.

Question: You were influenced by their gender awareness. How do you transfer this to all Hotline counsellors?

We have discussed this at the Hotline twice. Analysing Hotline cases from both a traditional and a feminist perspective, we have compared our possible responses from each of these perspectives. But I feel that our standard is still lacking. We will continue to make an effort and our gender awareness will become gradually stronger.

I took part in a discussion on a television programme recently. When the programme was broadcast, very little of what I had said was included, except for about two sentences. The bulk of what the ACWF person (with whom I had the discussion) said was included. We talked

---

11. The MWPCC Marriage and Family Research Project Group (*Hunyin jiating ketizu*) – Wang Xingjuan, Wang Fengxian, Rong Weiyi, Liu Ying – was involved in collaboration with the Department of Social Work and Social Administration of the University of Hong Kong to analyse Hotline cases.

about 'henpecked husbands'[12] – you know, very severe wives who control their husbands at home. The ACWF person thought they exist and that some women, who are not doing very well in their careers, react by being bossy at home. I do not agree. The reason for the appearance of this concept is that in the past women had no right to speak at all in their homes. They had no option but to listen to their husbands. Now women have their own jobs and equal status. They express their views at home and this leads to the concept of the henpecked husband. Originally, men didn't do any housework. Now men are required to take part. This is only reasonable. Both have jobs, so why should the wife alone be responsible for housework. Men do a tiny bit of work and then accuse their wives of making them into henpecked husbands. I think this is wrong. Husband and wife should be equal. There is a lot of domestic violence – you need to look at the whole context. But the television programme excluded my opinions.

Feminist ideas (*nüquan de sixiang*) have only recently entered our heads. This is not like in the USA or the UK where these ideas already have a long history. For us this is all very new. (Wang Xingjuan, interview 1998)

Structural factors – surviving as a 'popular' organization

An important defining characteristic of a popular organization (or NGO, the term that activists also apply) as used by both Wang Xingjuan and WRI/MWPCC activists is the fact that the organization receives 'absolutely no financial government support'. Because the WRI was a bottom-up initiative set up outside of any established organization or institution, a supervisory unit (*guakao danwei*) was needed to obtain formal and legal registration. When the WRI was set up in 1988, it became affiliated with the China Academy of Management Science (Zhongguo guanli kexue yanjiuyuan), a popular organization, which was in turn (until 1990) affiliated with a party-state institution. One of the benefits to the WRI of being formally affiliated to another popular organization was that the Academy, as the supervisory unit, did not attempt to control WRI activities. However, there were also disadvantages. For example, in 1993 a training workshop for Hotline counsellors with experts from the USA and Malaysia was held, and in 1995 the WRI invited non-Chinese speakers

---

12. The Chinese term is *qiguanyuan*. This literally means 'inflammation of the windpipe' and is a homonym for 'strict management by one's wife' (Honig and Hershatter 1988: 257).

to the NGO Forum workshop, and in both cases the supervisory unit did not have the authority to issue the invitation letters needed in order to obtain visas for the guests. In these cases, as well as in those in which papers needed processing so that activists could travel abroad to attend meetings, the WRI had to find other institutions which were willing to step in to provide the necessary administrative formalities.

In 1996, affiliation with the China Academy of Management Science came to an end. In connection with the Women's Conference, the WRI attracted the attention of the Public Security Bureau, since several foreign magazines and newspapers, as well as television and radio stations, came to visit the Institute. Wang Xingjuan laughed sardonically when she described how she and other activists felt that the many media visitors treated them like animals in a zoo. More problematic was the fact that she did not know what they were writing about the WRI, as journalists generally did not send copies of their coverage to the Institute. Moreover, the Institute had been accepting visits from journalists without undergoing application procedures, as they had not been notified of these and were unaware of their existence. The situation was exacerbated by the fact that some high-ranking political leaders and their wives, who were coming to China to attend the Women's Conference, made requests to visit the Institute. Among these were the Swedish Prime Pinister and US First Lady. As a result, the Security Bureau filed reports to high levels of the central government and began to investigate the work and registration situation of the Institute. Under these circumstances the supervisory unit terminated its agreement with the WRI and the Institute was asked to vacate the building which housed its offices. It had great difficulties in finding a new place (Wang Xingjuan 1999c and Wang Xingjuan 2000).

For some months it seemed that the organization might not survive, as it was no longer registered and had no premises. However, due to stubbornness and inventiveness on the part of Wang Xingjuan and other activists, it was transformed into the Maple Women's Psychological Counselling Centre late in 1996 and registered as a service enterprise (*fuwu qiye*).[13] Wang Xingjuan has explained what took place:

> When we tried to find a new place we could not even get any rental contract signed. The Public Security Bureau intervened in such a

---

13. The MWPCC registered with the Bureau of Industry and Commerce, Pinggu county in Beijing Municipality as an independent legal institution.

way that we would have no way to survive. How did we manage to pull through this difficult situation? Many people, such as Xie Lihua and Liu Bohong tried to help us to find a new supervisory unit for our organization to be affiliated with. During that time, I really became stigmatized and ostracized. No one wanted to have anything to do with me. I was accused of two offences. The State Council issued a circular that said that this was an infiltrating site of capitalism. This was how our organization was defined at the national circular. They asked why foreign organizations provided funding to my organization. Why did Hilary Clinton choose to visit our organization. This was all very difficult. How did we eventually solve the problems? We took advantage of the cracks and weak points in the system. I knew that there was no chance of registering as a social organization. So I contacted the Bureau of Industry and Commerce in a remote Beijing suburb. It was part of a suburban developing zone. This means that for five years we could operate without paying taxes. In this way I managed to secure a legal status for our organization. We became a service enterprise and as a legal entity we were registered with the Bureau of Industry and Commerce. Secondly, our country's democratic system is indeed making persistent progress. Even offices such as the Public Security Bureau have set up an Office of Appeal for individuals to vent their discontent. I sought them out to present my case. Within a week the Office sent me a letter of reply and they phoned me. They said that they thought what I was doing was rather good, and that there was nothing in the rules and regulations that prevented any citizen from meeting with foreigners. I recorded and transcribed the phone conversation. I circulated the transcription all over the place. I also went and asked to meet with the director of the Political and Legal Bureau of Beijing. They sent a chairperson to meet with me. He eventually stated, 'What you're doing contributes to the stability and solidarity of society. The Party and government support you.' I took notes of our conversation, and then took the notes to the Beijing Public Security Bureau. The bureau eventually had a formal meeting with me, and asked me to present my case. I took the chance to detail all the difficulties we had gone through over the years. In the end, I got their support. They apologized to me, 'Please understand that our duty is to protect the security of our country. So, if we have offended you, we trust you can understand.' This was the final agreement we came to reach. My activities and my organization are now approved by the Political and Legal Bureau of Beijing. I have also used my personal resources. Because of my work, I was nominated and awarded as an outstanding retired cadre by the Propaganda Department of the Party Committee of the Beijing municipality. Therefore, I often show people the award and title. I, as a party member, would never act against the nation. Once they had understood the work our organization is engaged in, they accepted and supported our work. This support is extremely important. (Wang Xingjuan at the 'Women Organizing in China' workshop, University of Oxford, July 1999)

℘ Lack of funding and staff

Activists in popular women's organizing talk of the structural diffi-culties confronting them in terms of three or four 'shortages' (*sanwu* or *siwu*). The exact definition of these 'shortages' varies, always includ-ing shortage of funds, but otherwise mentioning a combination of shortages of personnel, office space, appointed researchers or time for research (Jaschok, Milwertz and Hsiung 2001: 14). WRI and MWPCC activists concur that funding is the most difficult problem to solve in running a non-governmental organization. When they set up the Institute, five of the initiators contributed 20,000 yuan out of their personal savings to cover rent, office equipment and other expenses.

> When the WRI was first established, its office was located in a six-square-meter room in a one-story building, housing a primary school. There was space only for two face-to-face desks. There was no heating equipment except for a honeycomb brique stove. There was no telephone. In winter, biting winds blew into the office through the windows; in summer, desks and chairs were soaked by rain leaking through the ceiling. Seven years later, the Institute now rents ninety square meters of office space, including a conference room and two separate rooms for the Women's Hotline. In addition, a computer, a printer, a photocopying machine, a fax machine and other modern equipment have been purchased for the office. (Women's Research Institute 1995: 1)

In the early years of the WRI, several attempts were made at raising some money to run the Institute. A 1998 account of the history of the organization states: 'In the initial period, WRI staff used *all their energy* on the struggle to raise funds.' Some relatively unsuccessful English language courses were held and a stall selling clothes for women and children was set up twice at fairs at the Beijing Exhibition Centre, but this initiative was also a failure. 'In the end, they made a profit of only 300 yuan, not even enough to pay for the salespeople's lunches.' In 1989 the WRI began holding training seminars for women cadres, and in this way managed to secure some funding to run the

Figure 4: Wang Xingjuan selling clothes to raise funds for the Women's Research Institute at a fair at the Beijing Exhibition Centre. (Photo: The Women's Research Institute)

Institute.[14] The WRI first received financial support from institutions outside China in 1992, when the Global Fund for Women provided a grant towards the establishment of the first Women's Hotline. The Ford Foundation has supported the second Women's Hotline, the Aging Women's Hotline and the Ark Family Centre.

The shortage of permanent full-time staff – a continuous problem for the WRI/MWPCC – is in part due to lack of funds for proper salaries. The time that volunteer activists are able to put in is mainly limited by the time demanded by their paid jobs. All research projects have been carried out by volunteers in their spare time, and all Hotline counsellors are volunteer activists. While some activists have been engaged for many years in WRI/MWPCC activities – some even from the very establishment of the WRI or from the start of the first Hotline – many also have left, thus creating a constant need to recruit and train new Hotline counsellors.

ଐ An activist's experience
Some problems created by a general lack of understanding and recognition of popular organizing in the early years of the WRI are

---

14. See also Wang Xingjuan 1995 and 1999a.

illustrated by the following experiences of one WRI activist as she recalled these in 1996:

> In 1993 I was invited to take part in a conference in Vienna. When I asked for leave from work the head of my department was confused. Was this trip work related or was I going on vacation? It wasn't vacation, but it obviously wasn't related to my job either. Finally, he was very understanding and said, 'All-right, you can go, but don't talk about this to anyone'. Usually, if someone travels abroad their employer will provide some money for a suitcase or for some clothes. Neither my employer nor the WRI provided anything for this trip. The Ford Foundation covered travel expenses, but no one provided funds to cover the additional expenses. My boss was confused as to what a popular organization (*minjian zuzhi*) was all about. That year I realised that my boss was actually not very happy about my WRI-related activities. Also I was very busy and my health was not very good, so I stopped doing research for the Institute. I still do some Hotline counselling. I still help the WRI, but I do not spend nearly as much time as previously.
>
> Outsiders – that is my boss and society in general – don't really support NGOs. There are very few real NGOs in China. The WRI is a real NGO. This means that we have not received any support from the government. Most NGOs – for example those linked to the Ministry of Health, or various associations are in fact government bodies even though they call themselves NGOs. The WRI does not receive government support in terms of funds or personnel – there is just no support at all. We see the WRI as a real NGO, but it is very difficult. People feel that there is no need for NGOs. The government can take care of everything. Why would we want NGOs? (WRI activist, interview 1996)

The impact of organizing

❧ Changing ideas and practices

As already mentioned, Hotline counselling attitudes have changed over the years and a feminist or gender awareness was being required of new Hotline volunteers by 1998. One counsellor mentions that it was not unthinkable that a response to a woman complaining about her husband's extramarital affair in the early years might be that her husband must be quite handsome and that she ought to be pleased and proud on his behalf, but it is unlikely that such a reply would have been condoned by the late 1990s.

Experience and exchange with women's studies and women's organizations in other parts of the world have played a role in

Figure 5: Training of volunteer counsellors at the Sino-British Hotline Counselling Seminar, March 1997, organized by Professor Marianne Hester. (Photo: Cecilia Milwertz)

changing activist perspectives and thereby also their practices. One Hotline supervisor explained how her visit abroad as part of the preparations for the Women's Conference made an impression on her thinking:

> This was the first time I travelled abroad and I saw many, many women's organizations and what they were doing. This was completely different from what I had imagined. A lot of my ideas changed. I had always thought the position of Chinese women in society was relatively high. I thought that women in the West – well, I did not understand this. But it has to do with what was made public. We met scores of women's organizations – we talked with them. I thought that maybe the differences were due to different social systems. Chinese women's organizations perhaps depend on the state to resolve women's issues. Western women's organizations depend on themselves to resolve problems. They have a great diversity of interests and they call themselves interest organizations. Women in different social positions are confronted with different issues so they have different organizations. They all strive to protect their own rights and interests. They use many different methods. It seems to me that this is not what we do in China. The ways of thinking are not similar.

I think the position of Chinese women has been quite high since liberation [1949], but that women have not realized what their position is. They have not really understood their own rights. I don't think I myself had really fully realized these, but because I have worked for the Hotline, I feel that I have achieved new insights. My way of thinking has changed.

Question: Is this because gender equality in China was carried out from top to bottom?

Yes. But I think many people would not quite agree with my perspective and perhaps the government would not quite like this attitude. I think liberation of women in China was given to women by the Party. But women themselves really were not aware of what had happened. So according to this view of mine the women's movement has a seventy year global history whereas women in China achieved this position of equality very easily and have only understood this relatively slowly. Many women outside China have gradually, gradually fought for equality, so their awareness of that equality has also gradually developed. The improvement of their position and the development of their awareness have happened simultaneously. In China today those who really are aware of women's position are people engaged in women's work, but not the huge majority of people. So there are many women who say 'I really don't think my position is lower than a man's'. This is because they already have quite a high position.

My strongest impression from going abroad is that Chinese people like to talk. But they don't like to act. They like to talk and to write. But not to do very specific things. In other countries I experienced women's organizations who were engaged in very practical matters. We have only very recently started to do something similar in China, such as for example providing literacy classes. In the past, we just assumed that the State would take care of such matters. Chinese women's organizations are established by intellectuals, such as Chen Yiyun and Wang Xingjuan. They are academics – people who have become conscious of women's issues. Chinese women have not said 'I want to start this kind of organization myself'. Women have not set up organizations for themselves, for their own interests. Now it is only women who organize to help other women. Not women who start an organization based on their own needs. In China we just don't seem to do this. (WRI activist, interview 1996)

There was very little media coverage of the Women's Conference NGO Forum in Chinese media. However, activists spread their experiences of the Women's Conference, the NGO Forum and other visits and encounters with women's movements in other parts of the world via other channels. Those who teach, typically at universities, spread their knowledge to their students. At one university, the Women Professors' Association (Nüjiaoshou lianyihui) asked a WRI activist teacher to give a talk on her experience in taking part in the NGO Forum, as they knew practically nothing about the NGO Forum and Women's Conference. Following the first talk, they asked the activist to take part in future planning of their activities. Although the WRI/ MWPCC itself is not a national organization, activists believe they have a role to play in influencing people in all of China, because they can help individual Hotline callers and thereby spread new ideas and knowledge to people all over the country. Knowledge and new understandings are also spread beyond the Hotline through training courses. The Hotline provides data for research, and the research in turn leads to new ideas and practices for social support and training of MWPCC volunteers. This in turn created a basis for hotlines throughout the entire country via a nationwide hotline network established under the sponsorship of the MWPCC. More than fifty hotlines are part of the Network, and in April 1999 the MWPCC convened an international Seminar on Hotline Counselling (Xinli zixun rexian guoji yantaohui) for the network.

ℰℐ Policy recommendations

WRI/MWPCC research reports have led to recommendations to policy-makers with a view to improving the conditions of women's lives, and Hotline related research on marriage, domestic violence and sexual harassment has led to legislative proposals being put forward by the WRI. In 1996 a report analysing all Hotline calls on legal issues which came in between September 1992 and June 1996 was submitted to the Special Group of Women and Children of the Committee for Internal and Judicial Affairs under the People's Congress (*Quanguo renmin daibiao dahui neiwu sifa weiyuanhui funü ertong xiaozu*). The main objective of the proposal was to provide specific regulations to some clauses of the 1992 Law on the Rights and Interests of Women in order to promote implementation of the Law. The proposal included definitions of 'ill-treatment' and 'sexual harassment' and suggestions for legislation on domestic violence (Hongfeng 1998: 47–49). The Special Group recognized receipt of the proposal and replied that the proposal would be taken into consideration in revising and drafting laws.

In 1998, looking back at ten years of activism, Wang Xingjuan believed that the WRI/MWPCC had been able to influence policy-making to some extent;

... and this is what we strive to achieve. But can we actually do so? First of all, I think that the role of non-governmental organizations in society will gradually be acknowledged and the government will gradually have to formalize the conditions for these organizations.

You asked me about the role I have played and about what the role of the WRI has been. First of all, this leads to the question of society's acknowledgement and support. If we cannot achieve the recognition of society then the impact of our work, the influence, will be very small. We have reached some of our goals in the sense that the viability of future women's organizations will be indomitable because they match the trends of social development. The development of society needs this kind of popular organization. Government institutions are being reformed and reduced. In future the government will mainly be responsible for policy-making. But who will be responsible for the bulk of social work? This will not only be the government and the ACWF. Society is changing rapidly and many new contradictions are appearing. These need to be addressed. If they are not resolved society cannot advance.

Why do I say that the viability of women's organizations is very strong? Because society needs these organizations – such as for example our Hotlines – there are so many women who need them. So I feel that they have caused many government departments to gradually recognize that they can draw support from this strength, and that they need to draw support from this source of strength.

My aim is that society will gradually understand us and our activities. In the end the government will inevitably change its attitude. You asked whether our aim is to influence policy making. We have done a lot of work. However, how much impact this work has had – I do not dare to say. I can only say what we have done. I feel that the most important thing is that the government cannot ignore our existence. Society has to acknowledge the value of our existence.

In the very beginning, in 1988, the ACWF acknowledged the WRI. Then there was a period of – well, you know – and then they acknowledged us again. Their attitude to popular organizations has continuously been one of alternating between approval and denial, approval and denial – it is such a process. This process is very natural. So I am quite unperturbed. When they recognize our work I am really happy and I feel that we have gained more strength. And when they don't, I am able to understand and I make an extra effort. In the end I will make society realize that the work of Wang Xingjuan's organization is worthwhile to society – that we are making a contribution to society. (Wang Xingjuan, interview 1998)

3

The Jinglun Family Centre

This chapter describes the setting up and development of the Jinglun Family Centre in the form of a one-person narrative. The narrative is selectively pieced together and it is based on seven interviews with Chen Yiyun over a four-year period (1994–98). As such, it is an artificial construction. Some of the interviews went back in time to events that took place in the years prior to the establishment of the Centre. In each of the interviews we talked about what had happened recently, what was happening just now and what was going to happen in future. An event that was 'present' in one interview would be 'past' in the next. In the narrative, events in the past, present and future in terms of 'interview time' are conflated. When Chen Yiyun refers to specific moments in time and mentions 'now', 'last year' and so on, the year is inserted in brackets. The narrative is constructed to reflect the process of the development of Jinglun Family Centre priorities, strategies and practices, and the values that underlie these, rather than specific time. Therefore, not many specific dates are mentioned and the narrative is not consistently chronological.[1]

Counselling – finding the people with problems

In 1988 when I returned to China from my second visit to North America I wanted to engage in research in order to know what the reality of people's problems were. I spent a year abroad, and before I left I had read many stories in Chinese newspapers about marriage

---

1. I am indebted to Wang Zheng, as I was inspired to construct a single narrative based on several interviews after reading her book on women's movement activists in 1920–30s China (1999).

51

and sexual problems and about extramarital relationships. In addition to the stories there were statistics. I looked at all the numbers and thought they were extremely boring. They didn't illustrate anything. We write these ridiculous papers at the Academy. I have also done this stupid kind of thing. These texts have two functions: we academics need to prove that we are qualified researchers; and we need to earn money from our articles as a subsidy to our low income. These two functions are important to academics. If you don't publish you perish. Also, there is a real need to earn money. When I returned, I felt that I did not need either of these two. Financially I felt that my needs were covered by my husband's and my own income. And academically, well – of course I needed to continue writing, but I found that often our papers do not answer the questions many people ask. So I thought I would write papers that people liked to read and that I myself found interesting. There was a big gap between the stories and the numbers that I wanted to fill in. So, when I returned I thought, I will find the people with problems. Where were they? I did not know. Who were actually these people with the problems mentioned? The numbers said that 20 per cent had psychological problems and problems in interpersonal relations. But who were these percentages? I wanted to know who they were. Were they intellectuals, workers, peasants, young or old?

Before my second visit to North America I had started writing articles to express my views on marriage and family issues in popular magazines such as *Hunyin yu jiating* [Marriage and Family], *Jiating shenghuo zhenan* [Family Life Guide], and also in *Zhongguo funübao* [China Women's News]. My writing was based on a social work perspective. This was a new approach in China where you usually find two types of papers and talks: the theoretical academic ones; and those that are based on facts. I presented an analysis of empirical facts and cases. My approach was both practical and academic. You could place my approach somewhere in between what academics and social workers do. The media like this and journalists find it useful. They want analysis, but it needs to be an analysis that readers can make sense of – in other words, not too theoretical. Generally, media people consider me a very good writer. Unfortunately, these articles did not really reach a lot of people.

Then I had an opportunity to give some talks on the radio. I was invited to take part in a meeting held by *China Women's News*. At the meeting a case concerning a rural woman, whose husband had become disabled due to an accident, was discussed intensively. Should she divorce him? Should she remarry and bring him with her into her new marriage? These were some of the questions that were posed.[2] One of the many journalists at the meeting was radio journalist Wang Yongchen and she invited me to give some talks on marriage and family issues on the radio. At that time I had not done very much research but I was observing these issues. The divorce rates had increased since 1980 and she asked me to present my views on this development. I had a very superficial understanding at that time but there were very strong responses to the programmes and many people responded by sending letters to me.[3] Until then I had not known what to do with the letters people sent me. I could only send my replies to them. While I was in the USA I had been introduced to social work and counselling and now I wanted to try something similar. I thought I could do some face-to-face counselling because sometimes it is difficult to express things clearly in a letter. So I chose some letters from people in Beijing and I invited them to meet with me. I asked students, workers and intellectuals. I discovered that there were many problems. These people had not talked about their problems, mainly because there was nobody they could talk to, and also because they thought that their problems were private and that no-one else had similar problems. The problems I encountered were related to divorce, housing, abortion, violence, conflicts between students and their parents, and numerous extramarital affairs.

This is how I started my counselling. I have been engaged in counselling since 1988 – in my home, in my office, everywhere. I found a small bookstore where I could do counselling upstairs. Since 1993 we have had a small office. Actually, it was not counselling but more like chatting. Some people came and told me their stories. My goodness, how they talked! I don't feel that I could have collected so much information from the questionnaires I used to do. I talked to them as part of the data collection for my research and wrote up several cases, but they were not published: I had agreed that the conversations would be confidential.

---

2. The piece on Chen Yiyun in Wong (1995) elaborates on this meeting held by *China Women's News*.

3. Following the radio programmes, Chen Yiyun's talks were published in a booklet together with both a series of talks by Liang Jun (a scholar active in setting up the first women's studies centre in China in Zhengzhou, Henan Province) and a series of talks on 'How we can be fathers'. See Zhongyang renmin 1989.

Some time later, during the demonstrations in the summer of 1989, a strange thing happened. The national radio was not producing ordinary programmes, and they broadcast those radio talks [from the talks recorded in connection with the meetings organized by *China Women's News*] several times – at least three times – because they were not political. In this way, a great many people got to know me!

Chinese people have this very special characteristic that if they believe in you they will seek you out. After having listened to me on the radio many people thought that I was someone they could trust and many wrote to me saying: 'Why did I know nothing about you until now? I have heard you on the radio and I really liked your voice. I feel that you can certainly help me, so I want to talk to you if our conversation can be confidential.' Previously, there was no confidentiality if you contacted the Women's Federation, and people were afraid of being exposed. This is one reason that they wanted to see me. Another reason was that since I am an academic, many people consider me to be very trustworthy and they believe in me. The stories that I heard were very complicated, and sometimes if I talked to both the wife and the husband, their stories would be contradictory. It was extremely complicated to know who was telling the truth. I wanted to do research on this, but then I saw how pitiable each person was. Some wanted to commit suicide, some were ill, some women were going through their menopause. I thought that these women's problems were related to their physical states, not only to their husbands. They did not know anything about their bodies. I wanted to help them. Some women wanted to divorce their husbands due to some minor incident. I asked them if they had menopausal symptoms. I asked if they were very upset or angry or depressed, and I told them that their problems might actually be partially physical. There was no information at that time on middle-aged women, and I thought I needed to help them. Otherwise they would get a divorce, but their problem would not be solved. They were in a special period of their lives and needed to understand this instead of blaming their husbands or children. I thought that a lot of social work was needed.

I felt bad when I talked to them and then just let them leave. I felt I was using them, just writing my papers but otherwise not concerned about them. So I wanted to keep in touch with them. At first I did not know what to do to help them. Nobody had explained anything to me about my body but I had read books. When I studied at the Social Welfare School of the University of California, Los Angeles, I was introduced to counselling. I went to seminars and took part in discussions on counselling and social work, so I knew that these issues could be attended to by social work. But in China there was no social work, so I searched for social work practitioners. I didn't know whom to ask. I looked to the Women's Federation but they didn't seem to be doing this kind of work. The Women's Federation is mostly concerned with legal matters – with fighting in court. But many people need help for something other than a court case. They have psychological problems. But psychology in China is mostly a matter of research. The concept of mental health is also very new in China. If you say to someone in China that they have a mental health problem, they will reply 'I am not crazy'. They will think that you want to send them to a mental institution. So there is a big void in this field, with nobody doing anything. But if you want people to start doing something in this area, you have to explain to them why it is necessary. That's why I thought that this was not something I could do. I thought that I would stick to writing papers. But once I had talked to people, they wanted to see me again, because it was confidential – besides, Chinese people have confidence in authority. They think: 'since you are an academic, I want to hear what you have to say because it must be true.' Thus, I had to be very careful, as it could create a lot of trouble if I said something incorrect. This pushed me to study and read more books to find differences and similarities between the books and China's reality. There are many differences. I started to study social work, social psychology, books on environment and behaviour, psychological development and Freud: I started to look more closely into psychology.

The beginnings of an organization

In 1988 I set up a club for singles at the China Democratic League (Zhongguo minzhu tongmeng). It was the first club for single people in Beijing as this was before Wang Xingjuan set up her club. I am a member of the Democratic League and at our meetings I would give talks about marriage and family issues. Then some single men and women asked me to set up a single people's club. We placed an advertisement in *Beijing Evening News*. It said something like 'teacher Chen Yiyun of the Democratic League has established a singles' club. If you want to take part bring your identity card and proof that you are single'. They printed this advertisement without asking for payment – you see, this was before everything had become totally commercialized, and besides, I used to write for the newspaper. This was before the Jinglun Family Centre was set up, and it laid a good foundation for the establishment of the Centre.

After the advertisement in the newspaper 500 women and 300 men turned up. At first only ten people had joined the club and then twenty and then two hundred. But this was before we advertised. Then 800 were interested. We managed to find a big meeting place, but then June Fourth happened and we could not meet.[4] Too many people assembling at once was impossible. Also, the Democratic League building is at Xisi right near the Public Security Office, and they were keeping an eye on us because I had also asked some foreign friends to take part in Club activities and I had asked some Americans to give talks. I also invited Pan Suiming (who is a sexologist at the People's University) to talk. I brought in many experts. I asked them to talk about sexual and psychological issues. Many men came, too. We also discussed politics. We discussed many, many topics. We required all participants to have a college degree, because this was a cultural circle, and people communicate more easily within the same cultural circle. The Democratic League is also an intellectual organization and our activities were supported by the League. We used their assembly hall and the League did not want just anyone to enter. Everyone was checked at the door – so we had this requirement. After we had advertised we only held a few meetings and other activities, and then, because of June Fourth, we stopped. The League leadership talked to me and advised me not to continue – it was too dangerous. After June Fourth, Wang Xingjuan established her singles' club. I believe it is a commercial activity which is quite good. I introduced the new club to members of my club and they moved to the new club. Wang Xingjuan invited me to act as advisor to the new club together with Xie Lihua. I would go there about once a month to give a talk. Gradually I stopped doing this when I started the Jinglun Family Centre, but there are still people I know from then who come to talk to me when they have problems that they want to discuss.

Gradually more and more people started to contact me. Some people would even call the Institute of Sociology and say they were members of my family in order to get through to me. Others would turn up at my home from Guangdong, Hunan, Shaanxi and other provinces. I really did not know what to do. They did not have a lot of money and could not afford to stay at a guesthouse. Sometimes I let them stay at my home and sometimes they would stay on for many

---

4. The June Fourth [Incident] refers to the dramatic confrontation between students/workers and the leadership, which took place in the months up to and culminated on 4 June 1989.

days. In 1991 a student of mine and I were involved in a World Health Organization AIDS study at a re-educational institution for prostitutes in Guangzhou province. We interviewed fifty-six women and carried out a survey on sexually transmitted diseases. I was extremely shocked. Most of the women said that they would go back to working as prostitutes when they were released from the re-educational institution. Only seven said that they would stop and I gave them my card and told them to contact me. Two of them contacted me half a year later when they were released. One was from Guizhou province. She asked for money and I sent her 300 yuan. The other was from the Northeast and she travelled through Beijing on her way home. Her story inspired me to set up 'classes for girls' later on. Her stepfather did not treat her well, so it was difficult for her to return home and she wanted to stay in Beijing. She had no money and no identity card, so she could not stay at a guesthouse.[5] In the end, she stayed with me for three weeks. I found a job for her as a shop assistant but she was not satisfied with the pay. She was used to taking taxis regularly, so the money she earned did not cover her expenses. I gave her some money but she spent it immediately. She was twenty-one years old. My daughter gave up her room for her. Finally, she had to leave, and I bought her a train ticket. Later she called me and assured me that she would not take up prostitution again. She moved on to Shandong province to work for an earlier customer. She called me and wrote letters for about half a year and then there was no more news. I don't know what happened to her. I don't feel that I alone can follow up on so many people. I have the address of her sister-in-law and I have recently [1994] thought of writing to her but I have not yet written – I want to know how she is getting along now. I do not have time to write so many letters. I told people who contacted me to get in touch with their local branch of the Women's Federation. However, especially intellectuals are reluctant to contact the Women's Federation. I do not really know why. So I started to think that it was necessary to set up some kind of organization to help people.

Setting up the Centre

I wanted to find someone to do this with me but people would say to me: 'This is none of your business. It is Women's Federation business.' They said: 'You should not do this. These matters are the concern of

---

5. An identity card is required in order to register at a hotel or guesthouse and can only be replaced at the place of registered residency.

the Women's Federation, the Trade Union and the work unit. What in the world do you think you are doing by getting involved in all this, you cannot manage all this, after all there are too many Chinese people.' But I felt that I could not just ignore people's problems. I did not have the heart to close my eyes to people's problems. These people were the objects of my research, and if I turned my back on them when they had finished providing data to me, it would just be too heartless. This was my true feeling. I could not just let them drop away. I helped some people to analyse their problems and they told others: 'I have found a teacher who is helping me.' I truly felt that I could help some people. In other countries this is very common – but not in China. Psychology has not yet developed and people are not yet really aware of their emotions because China has concentrated on material survival for such a long time.

At that time [1988] China had just started to open up and reform. I wanted to set up some kind of centre but there were no such things as NGOs and there was no law to provide for them. I wrote a report to the Institute of Sociology. Then in 1989, you know, the June Fourth Incident occurred. Everything had been relatively relaxed, and then everyone started to be aware of politics again. So I hesitated. I did not know whether or not to continue. I decided to keep quiet for some time. Then regulations on NGOs were issued. In 1991 I wrote another report. This time it was to the China Association of Social Workers, which is registered with the Ministry of Civil Affairs. They responded: 'this is relatively complicated. First of all, you do not have any funds. Secondly, you have no office. Thirdly, you have no telephone.' At that time I did not even have a phone at home. They said that it would be very difficult. In 1992 I wrote again, and they said that the situation looked promising because now there were regulations.[6] I saw the Regulations in 1992 and I felt relatively confident because I would be able to register.[7]

---

6. In 1989 the State Council issued Document 43 – Regulations on the Registration and Management of Social Organizations (Howell 1994: 97). Mayfair Yang has noted that most people she spoke with during two visits to China in 1990 and 1991, did not know which office to go to for registration, nor what the exact procedures entailed (Yang, at a seminar at the Centre for East and Southeast Asia, University of Copenhagen, 1994, see also Yang 1994).
7. In April 2000, when Chen Yiyun tried to recapitulate the early attempts at registration she was not quite sure how many times, or when exactly, she had actually sent in reports. There may thus be some inaccuracy in the process as delineated here.

The Centre logo was created by an artist, and it was based on my idea. The black colour of the English word 'home' indicates danger and problems in the family. The red part of the logo is an old form of the Chinese character for 'family'. It shows a house or roof with people and animals within and symbolizes that the family constitutes a prosperous space. The combination of the black colour symbolizing problems and danger with a lot of red indicates that although there are problems the overall situation is positive. The Jinglun Family Centre is what its name indicates: a family centre. It is not a women's organization. We pay attention to the rights of both men and women. We aim at a gender balance among volunteers and the centre is not a feminist organization. The Jinglun in the name Jinglun Family Centre was originally constructed by combining the 'jing' of Beijing and the 'lun' of Duolunduo which is the Chinese for Toronto. This is because I developed the idea of a Centre in cooperation with Dr Danesh, who worked at a family counselling centre in Toronto at the time. I first met Dr Danesh in 1991 when he lectured at the Union Hospital in Beijing on the relationship between authoritarian families and adolescents. In 1992 Dr Danesh visited the Chinese Academy of Social Sciences (CASS) and I discussed counselling with him. Dr Danesh then suggested the establishment of a family counselling centre in Beijing, and I introduced him to the China Association of Social Workers (CASW). Our idea was that the centre in Canada would send experts to Beijing to train Jinglun Family Centre counsellors every year. When Dr Danesh moved to Switzerland in 1992, where he became the director of the Landegg Academy,[8] cooperation between Toronto and Beijing was discontinued and the 'lun' in the Jinglun Family Centre became instead the 'lun' from '*lunli*' which means ethics. This illustrates that the Centre works on family ethics.[9]

We registered as an NGO attached to the China Association of Social Workers (CASW). I felt that I could not manage this work on my own, so I invited a group of people to take part. I also needed a legal position. We could do this together. I was relatively fortunate because in 1988 when I returned to China, I was chosen as a standing committee member of the CASW. Thus when I set up the Jinglun Family Centre, I asked the CASW council to help me to set up a council. They suggested people such as Li Hongtao from the China

---

8. For information on the Landegg Academy, see www.landegg.edu
9. The character for 'lun' in Duolunduo – Toronto is identical to the character 'lun' in *lunli* – ethics.

Administration College for Women Cadres (Zhongguo funü ganbu guanli xueyuan), Xie Lihua from *China Women's News,* and Ding Hui, who is a medical doctor. I think this is really easy in China, not difficult as in your countries. When I contacted one person s/he would recommend many others. I also got hold of someone from the Women's Federation and Li Chunling from CASS and some doctors. I knew that there was a psychological counselling institute at Tongren Hospital and a psychological research institute at another hospital. At that time I was also chosen as standing committee member of the Mental Health Association of China, so I managed to find some psychologists there. It was very easy to find people. I also invited some journalists to take part. The journalists wanted to join me because they had interviewed me and published articles about my work. I applied for registration in 1992 and I registered in February 1993.[10]

Obstacles to organizing

In the beginning there were not really any obstacles. Only my employer, the Chinese Academy of Social Sciences, did not understand what I was up to. They thought I was engaged in business. They wanted to know if I was making money on the Centre. I don't think I can make any money as all services are free of charge. I have invested a lot of time and money. In the beginning many people did not understand what I was doing. At that time many people were 'jumping into the sea'.[11] They thought that this was what I had done too in order to make money. It was difficult for me to explain my motives. Perhaps it is partly due to my faith. My grandmother was a Buddhist and my father is a Confucian. They influenced me in the sense that many aspects of Confucianism are spiritual. I was educated as a child to serve people and sacrifice myself. I felt that if anyone needed help I should help them. This is an important incentive for my work. Without this philosophy I would not do what I do.

In 1990 I went to the Shenzhen Special Economic Zone to visit one of my brothers. He is a businessman and he had returned from Hong Kong. He really did not understand what I was doing. He wanted to offer me an excellent opportunity to do business in Russia since I speak both Russian and English and he knew someone in

10. The full name of the Centre is Jinglun jiating kexue zhongxin (Jinglun Family Scientific Centre).
11. *Xiahai* literally meaning 'jumping into the sea' is a metaphor for leaving the relative security of the state workplace to work for a private enterprise or set up an independent private business.

Russia who needed an assistant. He told me that I was exactly the person to fill the position and that the salary was quite high. He invited me go to Russia – my husband could go with me. But I hesitated. I did not have all the money I needed to rent rooms for my activities and to pay for the telephone – all of this is very expensive. But I could not go. I do not feel that I am good at business, besides, making money is against my values. My brother is quite bright. He studied at the People's University in Beijing but I do not think that making money has given him satisfaction in life. His business life is quite boring and he is often worried and anxious. I look at him and think, 'I do not want your kind of life'. But he thought that I let an excellent opportunity pass me by. In addition, the manager was 35 and I was already 49 – I did not want to be an assistant to a young manager. So I returned to Beijing and set up the Centre.

In the beginning I had no money. Then the China Association of Social Work (CASW) gave me 5,000 yuan. The CASW people are Ministry of Civil Affairs officials. They know me because I am a member of the standing committee of the CASW, so they had confidence that I would do good work. With this money I could go to the bank and open an account. When I had an account I started looking for a place and I applied for funding from the Ford Foundation. I received a grant from the Ford Foundation in October 1993. From 1988 until then I had used my own money. I had a telephone installed with my own money. I used my mother's money and my husband's money. From 1988 I had no funds and I never gave any of my salary to my husband. He was in charge of our household expenses, but he knew that I was not giving him my salary because I was using the money for my social work. When we had registered the NGO the group of people involved each donated a sum, as the 5,000 yuan from the CASW was not sufficient to cover our expenses. Each one donated 300–500 yuan until we had a total of 10,000 yuan. We wanted to rent an office, but were told that this sum would not cover one year's rent. Instead, a friend lent us a room in May–June 1993, a few months after registration. My parents were old and there was too much disturbance in my home so I needed another place to work from. The phone rang continuously. In November 1993 we received 74,000 US dollars from the Ford Foundation and we rented our offices in Dongchang Hutong. The grant was for two years' work. We chose to work in several areas and the grant covered two conferences, a youth education project, a women's counselling centre, grass-roots social worker training and the setting up of a shelter for victims of domestic violence.

Figure 6: Chen Yiyun at the Women's Counselling Activity House, the China Administration College for Women Cadres in 1994 with Li Hongtao and Zhang Lixi. (Photo: Kirstine Theilgaard)

The youth project was what we called a Girls' Club (Shaonü zhi jia) for counselling, meetings, activities and self-help groups. The name [which in Chinese includes the word home] symbolized that we wanted girls to feel at home and be able to speak openly about their problems. This project was done in cooperation with the Department of Social Work at the Youth School (Qingnian zhengzhi xueyuan), and their students acted as volunteers.[12] The Women's Counselling Activity House (Funü zixun yu huodong zhongxin) was a telephone and face-to-face counselling led by Li Hongtao at the China Administration College for Women Cadres (Zhongguo funü ganbu guanli xueyuan). The training of social workers was in cooperation with the Trade Union.

Addressing the issue of violence against women

We were engaged in many projects of which our work on domestic violence was just one. I wanted to collect some information; to test the water, the objective was to see what could be done, what we could tell the government and how we could influence public

---

12. See Long Di 1995 – a book for girls, based on the work of the Club.

opinion. Our aim was not primarily to help specific women. It was more that we wanted to know how serious the problem of domestic violence was. The newspapers had already addressed the issue. There was a big, shocking case that was brought to public attention by the Trade Union the early 1990s. The case concerned a man in Sichuan province who cut off his wife's ears and nose. It was first covered by the *Workers' Daily*. Someone from the Trade Union Department of Women Workers in Beijing travelled to Sichuan together with a journalist from the *Workers' Daily* to investigate the case. Later Tang Kebi from the Trade Union Women' Workers Department (she was also a member of the first Jinglun Family Centre Council) told me that the case was very serious. The man's work unit attempted to protect him by arguing that he was insane when he attacked his wife. However, the Department of Women Workers insisted that it was a criminal act and not a mental health problem. I think the Department takes the protection of the rights of women workers very seriously. Violence against women was a topic at the 1995 Women's Conference, but in China this is not something people know anything about. Our aim was to 'open the window' in the sense that we wanted to understand the situation and to engage in research and investigation. The objective was to inform the government, the Women's Federation and related organizations that this problem was very serious. We wanted to influence public opinion and make everyone realize that something is happening 'under the carpet'. We contacted a television company, presented the case to them and suggested that they should do a programme to start a debate about the problem.

There is a lot of domestic violence. I have knowledge of domestic violence especially in urban areas due to my counselling. Actually, originally we did not think that domestic violence existed at all. We thought that there was no violence in urban areas because since 1949 the Communist Party had taught us that everyone is equal. I think that we felt the benefits of that education and also believed that there was really no violence. But recently violence has increased. Through my counselling activities I have discovered that one of the reasons for divorce is that the husband hits his wife and child. I would ask women how their husbands could hit. 'Does he have a job?' They would respond: 'He does have a job but he drinks', and I realized that many people drink and then become violent. This has become worse since the reforms. Alcohol is a big problem. Many men become violent when they have been drinking. There are also men who feel lost.

They may have failed in a business transaction and then they become violent. Last year [1993] a study of 1,000 households in Beijing recorded violence in 20 per cent of them. In most cases, men hit women. There were a very few cases of the opposite. There was also violence against children. Teenagers complain of parents who hit them if their grades are low or they dress in ways of which their parents do not approve. Many young people have new ideas and lifestyles and there is an increase of generational conflicts now. In my opinion, our life used to be slow and steady. Now people are under pressure and they have no other outlet than violence within the family. They cannot very well hit a stranger, so they hit their wives and children. There used to be women who accepted their husbands hitting them, but now they say: 'We have had thirty years of equality and we will not accept violence.' I feel that the reforms have led to many changes and problems. Ideologically people are not ready to accept such rapid change and ordinary people feel lost. Inflation is high. We used to have security and welfare. For instance the work unit was responsible for medical insurance, but now people have to take care of themselves. And the competition is not just. People who do not have any 'backdoor relationships' are not in a good position. People's psychology is not stable. Now we have psychological issues rather than political issues. In the old days everyone was used to huge social differences. The rich were very rich and the poor were very poor. The common people were probably used to this situation. But we have had thirty years of equality since 1949, and then have suddenly changed to this stratification – people just cannot accept this rapid change. So I think China's situation is really special.

We worked with the issue of domestic violence for one Ford Foundation term from 1994 to 1996. We had applied for 10,000 US dollars for the project and we carried out an investigation and found a very secret place for a domestic violence shelter. There was lots of space. The place was also cheap and the building was even located quite near to a police station. We thought that this would make it safe. Actually, everything was just fine and we had reached the stage where we were planning on purchasing new beds and quilts. But after having done a lot of investigation we found that most people didn't think a shelter was necessary; nor did the Women's Federation approve. We had made contact to the local Beijing Women's Federation and to the Bureau of Civil Affairs, as we wanted to cooperate with them to set up the shelter. However, both said that it would not work. They said that if a shelter opened a lot of people with all kinds of problems would overrun the place. They were afraid of having to deal with a lot of people and they were afraid of dealing with the issue of violence. Actually, we had nearly reached an agreement and were about to draw up a contract when they withdrew their support. The leadership said that they had no prior experience in addressing the issue of violence. They were afraid of what would happen if violent husbands turned up at the shelter. They put forward a lot of reservations and we could not guarantee that we could solve all the problems. We held many meetings to discuss what to do. Should we insist on setting up a shelter? Our conclusion was that the Chinese situation is special and that every work unit can take care of you if you have a problem. It is not like in your country, where work units are not involved. The work unit dormitories have people who are in charge and they can protect employees. They have power. In addition, our basic community has not yet broken down. There are still functions that we can use. We need a shelter, but it is too expensive. Besides, a woman who is abused or violated can go to her parents' home or to other relatives' homes. Most people have some-where to go. Also, in China there are many helpful people: for instance, a prostitute stayed in my home. We can mobilize resources among the people. This is more warm. Abused women feel very lonely. Here it is not like in the US where there are many abused women together in a shelter. Here it would perhaps be one or two and they would be lonely and isolated. It is best for them to seek help from family or friends or their work unit and colleagues who can take care of them. We should take advantage of the Chinese socialist system. I think that this is better than to set up a shelter. In the end, we did not set up the shelter but instead we do work on prevention and education. We also had an emergency room in an underground guesthouse for half a year where we received three battered women.

The domestic violence hotline

In 1994 four organizations, the Department of Women Workers of the All China Federation of Trade Unions (Quanguo zonggonghui nüzhigong bu), the Department of Women Workers of the Beijing Trade Union, the *Workers' Daily* and the Jinglun Family Centre, co-operated to set up a domestic violence hotline. The Women's Federation tried to discourage us. They said that we should not do this and that domestic violence was a very sensitive issue. They felt that it was too sensitive and troublesome. I don't really know why they considered it so sensitive. Perhaps it is because this was just

Figure 7: Jinglun Family Centre illustrations used in training counsellors to handle domestic violence cases. (Photo: Cecilia Milwertz)

before the Women's Conference, and if we had addressed the issue of domestic violence at that time many people would find out about these problems and that might look bad. I think this may have been their reasoning because the Women's Federation is relatively political. I don't know if this was what they meant. In any case they advised us not to do this. We had planned to cooperate with the Beijing Women's Federation but they just said no to the shelter. We had discussed this with them for many months and originally we were supposed to start in March [1994] in cooperation with the Beijing Women's Federation. Then we turned to the Trade Union and we continued our negotiations with them. Why did the Trade Union have the courage to do this? I think perhaps because of my personal relationship with Tang Kebi. We have quite a good relationship. I persuaded her. I said: 'this is nothing serious, we are just going to talk on the phone.' The Trade Union would not have agreed to engage in a shelter either.

From the very first day when we advertised in the *Workers' Daily* there were many callers.[13] In the beginning the hotline was open 24 hours a day at the JFC office. So many people called. One phone was in the Centre office in the building where I live so I would also

---

13. The opening of the hotline was advertised in *Workers' Daily*, 14 October 1994, p. 8.

answer the phone.[14] There were phones at the Centre, at the newspaper office and at the Trade Union offices. Very soon we discovered that we could not cope with a 24-hour service because there were too few of us to answer the phone and we were exhausted. Transportation was an issue that we could not solve. We simply did not have the means to get people to the office. After the first month we changed our opening hours to 1 pm to 8 pm, and then the hotline functioned for about one and a half years.

One reason that we stopped the hotline was that we discovered that it was really difficult to run. For example what happened a few times was that the women who called were somewhere near the Centre. What should we do to help them when they told us that they were in a very dangerous situation? A few times we told them to come over to the Centre and we got hold of a doctor. But then once they were here, how could we ask them to go home? Most often, in these cases they did not reside in Beijing. They learned about the Centre from the newspaper and they turned up at our office. They would cry. We did not really have anywhere to put them up. We had a bed here so they could stay overnight, but I mean, the office only had two rooms. There was a woman who arrived from Hubei province. She had nowhere to stay and no money to pay to see a doctor. We arranged everything for her and we covered all her expenses. We discovered that ten helpers are not even enough to help one woman. Every day we had to care for her at the hospital. We just wanted to provide a hotline but there were problems that we could not disregard. We had to help. We really could not do anything else so we thought there should be a shelter in connection with the hotline; otherwise it was not really of any use, if you see what I mean.

This was the first reason that we found the whole situation very difficult and we discontinued the hotline. The second reason was that our budget was for two years, but by the end of the first year we had used up the funds. We had lots of expenses – medical expenses, taxis, investigation expenses – this was all very difficult. There was one very serious case, which was actually covered on television, of a woman who was beaten by her husband and pushed off the fourth floor of a building. We sent people to investigate, we collected

---

14. The first Jinglun Family Centre office, which still existed in 2000, was in the same building as Chen Yiyun's apartment. The second office, which opened in 1994 in addition to the first one, was located a few streets away from her home. This office closed in January 2000. Both buildings are owned by the Chinese Academy of Social Sciences.

donations for her and we sent clothes to her, as her husband had thrown away all her belongings. All this was very expensive. We just could not handle these cases. The Centre is very small. We discovered that it was relatively easy for the Centre to invite scholars to write and lecture, but very difficult to recruit people to take on concrete tasks. We needed someone to staff the Centre permanently. We do not have this experience in China. People do not have the training and do not understand the violence issue. So if we ask someone to take care of a domestic violence victim, they are afraid and no one will come. They will say: 'Oh, I don't do that kind of thing.' They need training to understand the issue of violence. If we do not have trained volunteers we risk hurting the clients – and they should not be hurt any further. But in China we have not had any training of social workers to deal with domestic violence. Scholars cannot just do this job. Our funds are insufficient and we cannot carry the responsibility for this training task. We also really lack people – volunteers. Many of the people who called wanted to come to the Centre or wanted us to come and investigate their cases. But we did not dare to receive them. What were we supposed to do once they were here? Finally, we discussed the matter with the Trade Union and agreed that as long as we did not have a very large budget we could not manage to work on the issue of domestic violence. Another problem was that most clients needed legal assistance, which the Centre could not provide. However, Pi Xiaoming had set up a legal aid centre and so had Ma Yinan and Guo Jianmei, so I thought we could transfer our clients to them. It was also a problem that in the beginning the Trade Union was very active in supporting the women but gradually there were too many cases. They could not cope. They had to prioritize employment issues and provide support for laid-off women workers.

We had plans to set up a Society for Research and Prevention of Domestic Violence (Jiating baoli yanjiu yu yufang hui) but we did not do this. We could not. One of the reasons I had to stop our domestic violence work was related to the case concerning the disfigured woman from Hubei province whom we had really made an effort to help. The case was covered by a major television channel in the USA. Then someone from the USA offered to pay for the woman to be treated there. The case became very sensitive. Because a foreigner wanted to receive this woman for treatment, the case would have to go through the Foreign Ministry. It gave the Centre a lot of trouble. You know, in China things like this are not simple. It became problematic because it could look as if the Centre was providing information on domestic violence to the foreign mass media. This would not be good for the Centre, so I decided that we could not continue to do that kind of work. The intentions from the USA were probably good, but in China the attention would only give rise to problems. So we stopped our domestic violence project both because it was too difficult and because it was becoming too sensitive. We discussed this with the Trade Union and they also thought we should stop and that we should not apply for funds from the Ford Foundation to continue this work. Some time later I saw a programme on television about a shelter in Shanghai but soon after it was also closed. The Jinglun Family Centre just does not have enough strength to take on this task.

Educational activities

I also feel that counselling only benefits too few people, so what I want to do is to try to use the mass media. We can respond to questions in the media and reach many more people. I started an advice column in *Marriage and Family* some years ago. I have also written a series of articles in a family planning magazine based on letters from readers. If I write a general article it functions as a response to many people. In China if you want to provide help in relation to problems that already exist it is not the same as in Denmark, where you have such a small population. In China there are so many people who need help and it all becomes much too expensive. It is impossible. We cannot afford it. So the best method is prevention. And the best prevention is education. When I say education, I mean in the sense of transmitting scientific information to people. I want to tell people the truth about how to protect themselves, how to adjust to market economy, how to support themselves and how to solve problems. In order to be able to apply self-help, self-knowledge is extremely important. In China lack of knowledge is a great problem. People do not understand. This is because China kept the door closed for so long.

As long as we engage in educational activities we can receive funding from foreign donors. As soon as we engage in intervention (*ganyu*), such as in our work on domestic violence, it becomes problematic because intervention involves contact with the victims. Victims are the dark side of social life. Education is positive. Problems are addressed but there is no direct contact with the victims. Newspapers can cover specific cases but we should only provide general scientific knowledge. We can address the background and causes of domestic violence and write about how to prevent it, for instance, how to teach equality and gender equality to children. This is very constructive. Education teaches how to treat people equally and discusses why men and women are different and why discrimination and abuse are wrong. We should provide education, including moral education, to children. We should provide values and sympathetic feelings and love and equality and teach people to treat everybody, not only their spouses, but also their children, parents and friends respectfully. I believe that we should start with education. We should not wait until someone has committed violence against someone else and then punish them. Then it is too late. I always say that the work of my centre in the past years [up to 1998] has engaged in many intervention activities, for instance providing counselling for victims of domestic violence or for parents who are having trouble with their children. In my opinion, since China is such a large country with a huge population, there will continuously be more and more cases. How many lawyers and how many social workers will we need to provide the necessary help? This is why we have moved into education for large target groups. I feel that the Centre has made the right decision in making this shift. We can reach many more people by providing education. Furthermore, in my opinion and also in the opinion of Centre experts such as Wang Jianzhong (head of a middle-school and director of a hotline for school children) and Wang Xiufang (a medical doctor), who are already broadcasting programmes on radio and television, we can influence even more people by using the mass media. The mass media don't like us to talk about too many victims or to address the dark side of society. I really feel that providing education is the best option. The media have huge networks that we can utilize to spread education. This suits the Jinglun Family Centre work especially well.

Cooperating with party-state institutions

We cooperate with the Trade Union, the Education Commission and local branches of the Women's Federation. We don't really have any relations with the central, national-level Women's Federation, but we do cooperate with the Association of Family Culture (Jiating wenhua yanjiuhui), which is associated to the Women's Federation. We carried out three nationwide training sessions with the Association of Family Culture – on marriage, family and gender issues – last year [1997]. All the participants were from the Women's Federation. In our work we focus on main points from the 1995 Women's Conference, such as reproductive and sexual health and adolescent issues

Figure 8: Chen Yiyun speaking at the 1995 NGO Forum workshop held by the Trade Union Department of Women Workers. (Photo: Cecilia Milwertz)

that were not included in previous Women's Federation training. Every branch of the Women's Federation has a Family Education Society (Jiating jiaoyu yanjiuhui) which is responsible for parents and children. So we provide them with knowledge on adolescents. Earlier on they were only concerned with pre-school children and there was a gap in terms of education for adolescents. The work of the Family Planning Commission was only targeted at married couples. We have tried to fill in the gap and promote education for adolescents. We have discussed the Centre adolescent education with the Women's Federation and they also feel that there is really a need for our education. The core content of Jinglun Family Centre adolescent education is concerned with sexology in a broad sense, including culture.[15]

Even though the Women's Federation and the Trade Union Department of Women Workers call themselves NGOs they engage in somewhat political and ideological work. They work primarily for the government. But I feel that in the period of reform, people are not especially concerned with political issues. You cannot use ideological or political methods anymore. What people need most is psychological or sociological work. There is a need to provide information to people in a scientific manner. The most important aim of my work is to provide scientifically based professional standard information rather than ideologically and politically based information. I feel that this is the most important difference between my work and that of the Women's Federation. During the Cultural Revolution science was defined in political and ideological terms. Marxist theory was very developed. But now Marxist theory is no longer sufficient. I feel that there is a need for additional perspectives focussing on behaviour, culture and the individual. In these areas science in China is not well developed, and since the opening of China and the reforms, many questions that face people are psychological issues – as for instance in personal relationships. In order to solve peoples' problems there is a need for new scientific knowledge within sociology, psychology, social work and sexology that goes beyond Marxism.

Values – scientifically based gender equality

If we look at the enormous problem of why women and men are not equal we have to acknowledge that there are biological and physical differences. But how can one think that intelligence is different for men and women? We need to approach this issue from a scientific standard. A test of children's intelligence carried out in Scotland determines that there is no difference in intelligence between boys and girls. We have to convey this to people. We have to explain how the differences are culturally and historically constructed. Based on scientific arguments we need to explain why we must have equality. In our talks and educational materials we address gender equality, women's participation and so on. The Women's Conference slogan was 'looking at the world through women's eyes'. We have an NGO perspective and a women's perspective in our work. But our per-

---

15. In 1997 the JFC published three books on sex education: Chen Jingqiu 1997, Chen Yiyun 1997 and Chen Yiyun and Wang Xiufang 1997.

spective is not quite identical to a Western feminist perspective in which there are some radical aspects that we might not be able to accept. There are attitudes towards divorce and women who do not want to marry in order not to become slaves to men. We do not agree with that. Also there are attitudes concerning lesbianism that we cannot accept. We do not mention lesbianism in our lectures, though of course if someone asks a question regarding lesbianism we will respond. But what we teach is probably not identical to what lesbians themselves would say. We believe that lesbianism is a form of biological preference that concerns a few people. They are struggling for their sexual preference. This is their own choice, it is not illegal according to our law and they should not be discriminated against. If they do not marry or if they cohabit – as long as they do not harm other people, for instance by having sexual relationships with under 16-year-olds and as long as they do not disrupt other peoples' relationships, then they are not doing anything illegal. Normal people should not discriminate against them. But for some people lesbianism is a lifestyle choice – and we do not support this. One cannot say that because one cannot establish a good relationship with a man one should choose to be with a woman. In my opinion we cannot accept this idea. If you are not biologically homosexual, but you want to demonstrate your very special unique lifestyle, well, I think this is a pointless choice. This is what we teach. If homosexuals choose to receive treatment, then as long as they are willing to accept the therapy it should be provided by doctors. This is what we teach. If students ask, we will respond but otherwise we do not include the issue of homosexuality in our lectures because the Jinglun Family Centre is engaged in social work. We are not doctors, and I feel that this issue is too specialized.[16]

In China the notion of women's liberation has been introduced by men. You know, many of the scholars who are engaged in research on women are men, so we do not emphasize that women alone can liberate themselves, or that women alone should solve their own problems. I feel that without liberation of men there cannot be such a thing as women's liberation. Women cannot be liberated in isolation. Traditional culture can be viewed as a chain that has tied both men and women. Traditional culture does not encourage men to do house-

---

16. The 2000 version of the Jinglun Family Centre 100 questions book includes a question on homosexuality. According to Chen Yiyun this was not written by her.

work or care for children. These are women's chores; men will lose face if they do them. Men have suffered a lot due to these ideas. Many men are losing their jobs now. So if the wife still has her job, then who is going to take care of the home? Why not men? I have written an article about men's liberation being the most important liberation challenge. Why have we been discussing women's liberation for 200–300 years, and why have women not been liberated? Because men are still not liberated from the chain of tradition. They have not realised that the chain of tradition also forces inequality on men. This is my view. I have written several pieces on this recently [1998], and I have also given several lectures. My personal opinion is that feminists criticize men and say that they are obstructing women's liberation, but men have not realised that they are also subjected to gender discrimination. So I talk not only from a women's perspective, but from both men and women's perspectives.

On the surface it may look as though men have power. Perhaps I cannot explain quite clearly what I mean. The reason is that I feel that at present, all sciences, including feminist science, argue within a material framework. They do not refer to the spiritual dimension. They look at who has the power, who has the material benefit. Within this framework I don't think that they will ever understand what is happening. Perhaps one can say that within the material framework, women can benefit from their subordinate positions. They don't have to risk their lives, so they live longer. Women are safe within the home while men make money outside the home. In this sense, I think men are not winners but losers. They sacrifice a lot and their lives are 4–6 years shorter than women's. If a woman loses her job and becomes a homemaker everyone finds this acceptable. But if a man loses his job then neither the men themselves, the work unit nor society as a whole can accept it. Why can't a man be a homemaker? It should be possible to consider what would be best for the family. For instance, if my husband and I were to decide that one of us should quit our job, then my husband does not have as much work as I do, so the effect on society would not be as great if he quit his job. But if my husband said 'I don't want to quit my job, you can quit yours instead', I would find this very bothersome. However, in reality it is not that my husband does not want to retire. He really wants to, but according to public opinion a man who returns to the home is without future. To me the important question is: 'Who is needed at home?' When my mother-in-law was ill and we needed to take her every day to see the doctor, well, I could not take her, so my husband

74

had to take leave from work to do this. My parents are in their 80s, and if they need physical help my husband is the one who best can provide this kind of help. This does not mean that because my husband takes time off from work, he has no value. This material world is constantly weighing your value – always asking you how much you earn, how much power do you have. Do you see what I mean? I feel that women have followed that way. They are focused on how much power one has in the political arena, how much money one can earn. Is there equal pay? Can you perhaps even earn more than a man? That means that you are successful. That means equality. For that you have to make many scarifices and you do not have time to care for children. You don't have time for motherhood. So there is a lot of sacrifice for both men and women in this world. I think that we need to change our perspective and look at what is happening with men *and* women – never separate the two any more. Men may seem to have a lot of authority in the political field but if you look at prisons you will notice that most prisoners are men. What does this illustrate? It illustrates that in order to keep power and get money, men have to fight. They even have to kill in order to be successful. They end up in prison – so all this is not beneficial to men.

Basic equality values

I find that many women go after power and empowerment. I don't like the term empowerment. Most important is a mutual understanding between men and women. So I think men need to be involved. The women's movement has made men very upset. Men have always felt that women were fighting them for power. So men have been very confused. For instance, victims of domestic violence are mostly women, but the majority of victims of social violence, such as killings and robberies, are men. One year I investigated the statistics of reported violence at a police station. This was at the time when the Centre was engaged in the issue of violence. They said that most victims of violence were women and children because they are physically or psychologically weak. Men are strong, but they are victims of social violence. In 1998 the Ford Foundation asked me to take part in a meeting in India on domestic violence because I had previously engaged in domestic violence work. I was interested to know how India and other countries solve these problems. After the meeting, I felt that nothing could be done. In India and Indonesia every year there is more and more talk of domestic violence. At the same time there is an increase in violence. I don't think you can solve the issue if you do not solve men's problems. Men beat their wives because they are stressed. They have to be successful – and if they are not they go home and beat their wives. If they are weak in relation to their bosses, then at least they can be powerful in relation to their wives. This is a very big problem. I think any person - man, woman or child - who is only interested in power will harm others. Basic values need to be changed. I don't think that market economy promotes values for a civilized spirit – it is a material thing and people become weak victims. I am reconsidering the existing situation, the existing order. When Clinton and Jiang Zemin talk, all they talk about is material issues – financial matters. I think that there will be even more financial storms. We will not solve these issues. Look at the present floods. Everyone is focused on economic growth – eight per cent, nine per cent – meaning that more earth must be dug, more trees must be felled, and there will be even more pollution. Everyone is just seeking power and money.

I support a basic-needs strategy. What are our basic needs for survival? How many clothes and cosmetics and how many cars do we need before it is enough? I think that we should have a strategy to satisfy the basic needs of ordinary people. I don't think socialism is bad, but – socialism has not been realised anywhere. Many people say that socialism is idealistic, but I believe we have to think about whether or not it can be realised, and I wonder which country or government will have the courage to experiment. Who will look at how men and women, children and mothers ought to live? I really feel that this world has become more and more evil. I mean, has capitalism succeeded? Some people are very rich but many more are poor. The material resources of the world are limited. It is unreasonable that a small percentage of the world's population consumes a relatively large proportion of resources. We need to change our way of thinking about the world, including gender. The idea of socialism is to liberate the whole society – women and men. I think this is correct. At the moment a lot of emphasis is placed on women's perspectives, women's feelings – I think women's feelings are the feelings of a victim or subordinate group. That is history and totally wrong – both men and women have been made into victims. We need to look at the world with the eyes of both men and women.

When we look at Western society we see identical problems. We have been to Denmark and Sweden and seen that many women live with other women and men are engaged in violence or drugs. I do not think the separation of men and women, divorce and women living alone with children is good. The children don't have their fathers. There are so many problems. Why are the relationships between people getting worse and worse? What is the reason? Why does no one discuss how we can build good harmonious relationships? It seems as if people just say – 'oh, we have some problems, let's get a divorce'. Perhaps peoples' expectations – towards men, towards society – are too high. And if the expectations are not realised, they just divorce. In Sweden I saw lots of children who had no fathers. Nor is it any good if fathers live with their children but do not have time to spend with them. This happens when the father is away from the home – making money and proving his success. These are material values. We have to change our values totally. This is the way we should educate our youth. If we do not change our basic attitudes, culture and way of life in order to build this world, men will suffer and women will suffer.

Do you know why men's average life expectancy is shorter than women's? Is this a biological or a social problem? There are both biological and social reasons for the shorter life expectancy of men. Men are engaged in more dangerous occupations than women, more men than women fight wars, more men than women die. Look at the present fighting of floods and provision of disaster relief – men are doing these. The risk that they will die is relatively high. In this type of dangerous activity everyone says 'oh, girls should not take part'. Is this not a reason that men sacrifice more? If they do not suc-ceed they cannot survive. For women it is all right. This is definitely not good. At the moment we are discussing with many men the actual benefits of inequality between men and women. Men think about their parents, about their fathers, about men in the political arena, about criminals in prisons. They think that there is a balance more or less – they lose and win. Losing is followed by winning and winning is followed by losing. There are many kinds of suffering. I believe we have to discuss new methods – how people should live in the 21st century.

Gender inequality used to be explained as a class problem. I believe that it is a question of traditional culture rather than a political and class issue. Gender inequality is not necessarily linked to economy and class. Upper class women are not equal. We have to explain that there is no scientific basis for inequality. Inequality cannot be explained on the basis of women's physical weakness. But no one used to say this in China – not even the Women's Federation. A change is taking place now, and there are people at the Administration

College for Women Cadres[17] who approach the matter of inequality in a scientific manner rather than a political one. There have been significant changes within the Women's Federation in recent years. But Chinese public life requires a great many professionals. When I started my work, the Women's Federation had basically not done this kind of professional scientific work. But within recent years they have also started doing so, and I cooperate with them.

Cooperation with the ACWF and the Trade Union

Our cooperation with the Women's Federation and the Trade Union started when we announced the birth of the Jinglun Family Centre (JFC) to them. We simply got hold of their directories and we sent out an announcement to them informing them that we were coming to this and this place at such and such a time to give talks. We sent them a list of topics. They could choose whatever they were interested in, such as for example a talk by Pan Suiming. They responded 'we would like you to come at such and such a date to talk to so and so many people'. Now they contact us. We do not need to send out announcements. Now we basically do not need to make contact – they contact us. They also came to know about us because we announced the setting up of the Centre in the media and because there was quite a lot of media coverage in the early years in newspapers such as the *Workers' Daily*, *China Women's News* and *Legal Daily* (*Fazhibao*). Both the announcements and the articles would have our address and phone number and they would contact us. We sent out announcements the first two years. Since then it has not been necessary.

In the beginning the Women's Federation did not know what the JFC was. Once a Women's Federation head of department called to ask about the Centre – what were we doing, when was the Centre established, and why did they not know anything? I am fully aware that there is a lot of competition and this is why I make an effort to cooperate. I have no intention of competing. After all, we are not engaged in business and this is not a matter of making money. Our resources are intellectual and their resources are a network. We ought to combine our resources. We should cooperate rather than compete. I don't quite understand their psychology but I do have a sense that there are people within the Women's Federation who

---

17. Since 1995 renamed as the China Women's College (Zhonghua nüzi xueyuan).

cannot accept some of the ideas that I present in my talks. Once, after I had given a talk in Tianjin a friend told me that someone from the Women's Federation had listened to the tapes. I had talked about extramarital affairs. I had said that it is unfair only to blame the third party and that you have to consider the relationship between the husband and wife. I think this person misunderstood me. She thought I was encouraging or justifying affairs when actually I was approaching the issue scientifically in order to present an analysis of the causes of extramarital affairs. I look at gender imbalance and structural imbalance. There are, for instance, well-educated, professional single women who are looking for a partner, but because there are not enough candidates they may end up having affairs with married men. So I was saying that men have more opportunities and choice and this may be one reason for extra marital relations. This misunderstanding happened in the late 1980s. Now I think most people know that what I say is correct and that we must apply scientific insight. More and more people share these ideas now. Of course, there are values involved in what I say, too, but they are different values from theirs. I also think that there are issues of ethics and morality involved, but first of all we need to focus on what is actually happening – what the scientific facts are. I am interested in how we can combine ethics and morality with scientific knowledge.

In all our educational activities we work with party-state institutions. We bring our ideas into the process of our cooperation and we influence them from below. Officials do not have any ideology concerning marriage and family. They need an ideology. The ideology they have is political and empty. When I talk to officials I talk about why it is important to protect women's health and why men need to participate in family planning, for instance, one official said to me: 'If a man is sterilized then he will not be able to work.' I told him that this is a misunderstanding. This official said that wives also believe that their husbands will lose their ability to work if they are sterilized, so to avoid the negative effects on their family economy, the wife will offer to be sterilized. I responded that on the basis of scientific findings, there is no evidence that men will lose their strength. I also explained the scientific facts of how one gives birth to a boy or a girl. People have not been aware of the facts. They would just say: 'This woman can only give birth to girls, so the man had better find another woman who can give birth to a son.' Many people know nothing about sperm and eggs and chromosomes. Of course, people in the family planning institution know, but some local officials don't know! So we address these topics as part of our adolescent education. We explain the principles of reproduction so that children will have this basic knowledge from an early stage. We aim to lay a good foundation for their understanding.

Providing knowledge and education

The main objective of the Jinglun Family Centre is to provide knowledge. Once people have knowledge their attitudes can change. We have cooperated with officials from the very start. I think this cooperation is very good. One of the advantages of Chinese society is that the official system has a complete network. If a women's organization in some other country, for instance the Philippines, wants to engage in community work it is very difficult to influence a large segment of the population. Because China has such a huge population, networks that reach out to many people are crucial, otherwise one could never hope to reach everyone. Networks are very important, and we use the official networks. Social life in China is very well organized and everybody is linked to a network. Nobody is missing. We can use these networks to reach everybody. It is an advantage that everybody is safely anchored within a network. At the same time it can be a disadvantage that everybody is controlled and that there is not much freedom. In China we need both safety and freedom, but I feel that if we lose freedom in order to achieve safety, this is unbalanced. Networks are very good for securing safety and providing information. This is a clear benefit of the Chinese system.

When the Centre was established the idea was not to set up a large organization, but to set up a small core organization that would interact with other organizations and departments to provide education. We have united experts from outside and within existing networks. We have integrated the specialists that were already within the networks with our own specialists. In June [1998] I attended a meeting with educational authorities in Shanghai. The State Education Commission Department of Moral Education also attended the meeting. We discussed the Jinglun Family Centre adolescent education and our books. When our two Shanghai-based experts and I had given our talks I felt that these people's attitudes changed. Then, yesterday, they sent someone from their publishing house to meet with me. They are compiling a series of textbooks for adolescent education and they asked the three of us to take part in editing these new educational materials. I think this illustrates that earlier they would only ask their own specialists to do this work, but after having met us at the Shanghai meeting they sent their representative to negotiate with the Jinglun Family Centre. If we can join them, we can spread our ideas through their textbooks. They print hundreds of millions of copies so there would be a great impact. Furthermore, the State Education Commission is planning a meeting to discuss adolescent mental health problems such as school pressure and the problems of single children, and they asked me to suggest some Jinglun Family Centre experts to take part in the meeting. Previously, the Education Commission had no idea of the mental health problems with which adolescents struggle. They thought that mental health problems only concerned adults. Based on Centre surveys and interviews with adolescents we can demonstrate that teenagers are often confused and in doubt. For instance, in our interviews we have asked whether teenagers have contemplated suicide. Have they been depressed, what other feelings do they have? We can report investigation results to the Education Commission and make them understand and recognize that mental health is a problem related to teenagers as well.

Within recent years the Education Commission has started to offer psychological counselling at schools, but as a government institution they do not have many people engaged in discussing these issues. My feeling is also that their own experts are not as daring in discussing these issues as Jinglun Family Centre experts can be. After all, we are outsiders, and thus we are not afraid of the consequences. We can be relatively objective. I think this is preferable. Furthermore, the Education Commission does not always pay much attention to the opinions of their own professionals. In this sense it is easier if one comes from outside the institution itself. This is a NGO function. When we address an issue from the outside we don't necessarily have to be afraid of any pressure. We are relatively free. China also has a psychological tendency to believe that outsiders or strangers make a great impact. This is a cultural habit. We have a saying that goes: 'The outside monk recites the scripture well.' This means that identical teachings are more beautiful when read by outsiders. China has very good technological experts, but somehow foreigners always seem to be preferred. I don't think foreigners are more qualified than Chinese. This a bad cultural habit, but at the same time it is a habit that we can benefit from in our work. Sometimes, in fact, I think that their own experts are more knowledgeable than we are, but they do not ask them to give talks. It may also be problematic for these people that their examples refer to their own schools. Perhaps if a counsellor says 'our school has many children with mental health problems', the Education Commission may react by saying: 'Then your school is no good.' So sometimes the facts are not brought out into the open. When a JFC expert gives a talk we never mention names of the schools from which our examples originate. This makes it convenient for us to give talks and for the Education Commission to invite us.

We also cooperate with the Family Planning Commission. We originally contacted them. We said that they should not direct their information only at married couples. We told them that our experience from schools showed that students really wanted and needed information. They can make mistakes out of ignorance. We said to the Family Planning Commission that they needed to take this into consideration. They responded that they could not do this as long as they were not asked to do so by higher levels within their own system. Later, we ourselves gave classes at middle schools in Shanghai, Shenzhen, Henan and Sichuan provinces. Articles were written about our classes in the local newspapers, and then local authorities contacted us. In Beijing the *Youth Daily* wrote about our classes for teenagers, and then local levels of the Family Planning Commission started contacting us. In Beijing the first was the Dongcheng District Family Planning Commission.[18] They had opened a population school and they asked us whether the curriculum should include education for adolescents and their parents. We answered that of course it should and they asked us what should be taught. We sent people to talk to them and now our experts give talks every term. Dongcheng District has a population of 600,000 and about half are school-age children. We give instruction to all children, except the youngest, as well as to their parents and teachers.

Centre capacity and resources

Our ability to exert influence is very strong. Now [1998] all big cities know about the Centre. There are people in Shandong and in Shenzhen who want to set up branches of the Jinglun Family Centre. In Shenzhen they mainly want to provide adolescent education and in Shandong they mainly want to provide counselling. I feel that the Centre is not strong enough at at the moment. We had a group of professionals linked to the Centre, but now some have left China and have not returned. Others, such as Hu Peichen – who is the dean of the Department of Psychology at Beijing Medical University,

18. Beijing Municipality is divided into a number of administrative districts. The Dongcheng District is one of four central city districts.

Li Zixun, medical doctor and psychotherapist, and Wang Xiufang are more and more busy. This is a big problem. They are very capable, but this means that they are also very much in demand. It used to be easy to ask them to take on assignments, but now it is becoming more difficult. This is really a problem. We need to recruit new people, but new people need training and time to adjust to a work process. We cannot send experts to places outside Beijing any longer. I have asked people from the Hong Kong social welfare department to help out in Shenzhen. In Shanghai they can take care of themselves. In Shandong, Henan and Tianjin, however, they are continuously asking for help, but we do not have the capacity to send people there any longer. One year, seven of us went to Henan to help them train people there.

We do not have the original group of experts any longer. However, others have joined us. Pan Suiming is too busy now. Besides, I do not agree with his Kinsey approach.[19] In some places such as Zhejiang province we have extended the group of experts to include local people. We have invited them in to save time and money. Just about every place has local experts who can join our work. But if there are only medical doctors somewhere, we send someone from Beijing, for instance Li Hongtao, someone from the People's University or legal experts from the Institute of Law at CASS. The group of experts is constantly changing. There have been changes every year. Some people are too busy, and if they have not attended meetings for a long time, we find someone else. Now [1997] the first Council is more or less changed. Only Long Di and Ding Hui remain from the original group. Just the two of them. Xie Lihua used to be a member of the JFC Council. She became too busy when she set up the *Rural Women Knowing All* magazine. She got terribly busy and did not have time.

The Council holds one or two meetings annually to plan our activities. Sometimes we extend the Council. Last year [1996] we invited some school presidents and leaders from the Education Commission and the Family Planning Commission to a seminar on adolescent education. They made many suggestions, the Council drafted our plans and we decided to publish three books. This year [1997] in February we held a council meeting to discuss the delegation to Sweden. Most of the Council went to Sweden. At present the Council is more or less identical with the authors of the books. The Council is an advisory body to the Centre. You could also call it an

---

19. See Sigley and Jeffreys (1999) for an interview with Pan Suiming.

academic commission. I am responsible for the day to day work of the Centre together with the office staff. However, it is very difficult. There used to be a group of volunteers who worked with me. Now there are none. Sometimes students from the social work course at Peking University do internships here. But it is difficult because what they have studied at the university and what I am doing are two different things. They have learned a lot of theory but no practice. They need practice, but as they are only here for very short periods of time, sometimes they just cause a lot of confusion. Their practice time is too short. Besides, they don't have the desire to do this work. It is just part of their course.

I want to involve more people, especially young MAs and PhDs from the Institute of Sociology, in order to raise the quality of the service. I think that now [1997] relatively many people, including the leadership, understand what I am doing. They support my work and some are willing to take part. We are preparing an international conference as a cooperative effort between the JFC and the Institute of Sociology at CASS, and a PhD student is helping out.[20] Li Chunling used to help out with adolescent education, but now she is studying for her PhD and is very busy. I have spoken with the Section on Family Studies at the Institute of Sociology about the possibility of them taking part in my survey and educational work. I want to invite scholars from CASS to give lectures for the Jinglun Family Centre, and I want to train some young people. I have discussed this with the director of the Institute of Sociology and he says that there are young people who do not have enough work to do because the Institute lacks research funding. These young people have some basic training and knowledge, so it would be better than trying to find volunteers outside. I want to train sociologists to pioneer this area. We have also discussed the possibility of simply registering the Jinglun Family Centre with CASS. Sometimes I have the feeling that China Association of Social Workers (CASW) does not really know or care what I am doing. They have many social-work delegations coming in from Hong Kong, but they do not contact me. Their social work is community work, so their concepts are different from mine. Actually, I feel very isolated. I often feel that no one is interested in supporting a small NGO. I am exhausted and I really need a supportive system. CASW is not very supportive because we do not do the

---

20. The 1998 Beijing International Conference on Family, Social Security and Social Welfare, 4–6 April 1998.

Figure 9: The Jinglun Family Centre office in 1995. (Photo: Cecilia Milwertz)

Figure 10: Jinglun Family Centre staff in 1995. (Photo: Cecilia Milwertz)

same kind of work. Furthermore, my full-time paid job is with CASS, so in a sense it would be more suitable to register there. I should sort this out next year. I have already talked to CASW about this and they agree. I will still be applying for foreign funds.

There are already two associations registered at the Institute of Sociology. One is the Association of Sociologists, so I could register under this association as an NGO, not as part of the institute. This association has many members all over China. There is also the Association of Social Psychologists. Both these associations are NGOs. Their members are not only from CASS; they come from all over the nation. The JFC could make contacts all over the country through them. This is my plan, and perhaps it will materialize eventually. If not, I may have to close down the JFC. I have too much work and I cannot continue like this. I just cannot cope in the long run. Neither my husband nor my parents approve of my present situation, as I am sacrificing my health. I sleep very little. There is just too much work and it is too difficult to find part-time help. For full time help you can only find retired people and they don't have the energy or capacity to do this work.

Li Guixin worked for the JFC for quite some time but she did not do professional work. She was responsible for management. She had originally been a librarian and she was good at managing our files, but she was not a very good manager. We have a very dependable and responsible cashier at the moment [1994–1997]. In addition, Xiao Hong helps out and there is a young man, Li Xiaopeng, who is helping with the international conference preparations. Lao Ye is in charge of our life education (*renshen jiaoyu*) exhibition and for planning lectures in connection with the exhibition. He used to be president of the Children's Welfare House (Ertong fuliyuan). He retired early. He is only 50 years old and very good at management. My sister Chen Jingqiu has helped out since last year [1996] when she came to take part in editing the books. She may take on part of my work. But still I need more people. I need people who will come in every day. Most of our counsellors are doctors and I am not quite satisfied with this situation. They are very preoccupied with illness. But our main focus is education and prevention. I must have people to take over after me. I cannot do this forever and I need to concentrate more on my research. I have given up several academic opportunities to travel abroad to universities both in the USA and the UK. They have invited me as a guest scholar but I have declined. I do not have the time. The Landegg Academy has invited me this year [1997], but if no one can take over my work, I cannot leave. I have so much to do and I don't have the time.

At the moment [1998] I am trying to set up a long-distance-learning university at CASS. I am negotiating with the Institute of Sociology to open two long-distance university departments. One is on social work and is in cooperation with the Trade Union. There is very little social work training in China. The other course is on gender and family studies. This is in cooperation with the Women's Federation Family Culture Association, which is an NGO under the Women's Federation. The idea is to teach over the internet. Then our experts will not have to travel. We can just make tapes and videos.

Review and plans for the future

We have applied to the Ford Foundation for funds to set up an information centre next year [1999]. And we want to publish a newsletter. The information centre and the newsletter will be a cooperation with the Sexology Association. The idea of setting up an information centre had developed because our resources are insufficient. We cannot travel anymore. In the beginning we would travel to Tianjin and Hebei, but now we have to go to places that are further away, such as Shenzhen and Shanghai. It is too far and too expensive. The information centre would enable us to write our ideas in books and newsletters and then send them out to all parts of the country without having to travel. We would not be responsible for the actual training workshops but only for the teaching materials. In this way we could cover a larger group of trainers. The JFC has pioneered this work and has sowed the seeds for many activities. We have planted and cultivated and harvested. We cannot do all this anymore. In future we will only plant the seeds. This year [1998] is a year of rest for our experts. Eight experts are engaged in an adolescent questionnaire survey, but otherwise we basically do not have any activities. Next year [1999] we will start the information centre. We will not have to ask people to actually physically come to the Centre. They can do their writing at home. Only in special cases, such as if we do a video, will we ask them to come for one or two days.

Two years ago [1996] I was worried about the future of the JFC. Then the conditions were complicated. I was registered as a CASS employee but the Association of Social Workers is part of the Ministry of Civil Affairs, so I thought they would close the Centre as part of the reorganizing that was going on at that time. Or perhaps, as the Ministry is very political, they would say that it was not good for the

Centre to be related to the Ford Foundation. But they have not criticized anything or pointed to any problems. The recent People's Congress stated that government policy would encourage more intermediate organs (*zhongjie jigou*) – I think this must have meant NGOs, but it was not very clear and I am not sure. Last year I was very worried. The CASW had said something about the Ford Foundation being linked to the CIA and there were rumours going on about a document concerning the Ford Foundation. But now I feel that the situation has improved. The Centre also has contacts to the Swedish International Development Cooperation Agency (Sida) and the British Council so there is more of a balance now – not only links to the Ford Foundation. If we set up the information centre it will be much safer as we will not be engaged in so many activities. People can decide for themselves what they want to do with our information – this is safer for us. I was also worried about financial matters. There were continuously more and more requirements and expenses but it was not certain that the Ford Foundation would provide more funds. The information centre will not have that many expenses for instance for travel and for hiring people. We will mainly have printing and translation expenses.

In the early JFC years, we did street counselling to make the Centre known. No-one knew about us so we had to publicize our activities. Then we had a period of training and teaching and now [1998] we are moving on to set up an information centre. We will also focus on the massmedia. Next year [1999] we will start a weekly programme on Beijing Radio. We have more and more cooperation with the media. Beijing Television runs a sex-education programme in cooperation with the Family Planning Commission and they have asked the Centre to take part. We also have cooperation with a national radio programme.

Over the years, a total of about sixty experts have worked for the JFC, about half in Beijing and the rest in other parts of the country. They have mainly been doctors, psychologists, educators, teachers and social workers. In the future we want to use the information network to set up links to even more professionals all over China. The main work of the Centre will be to edit a newsletter and produce educational programmes and have them broadcast by the mass media. We can also disseminate locally to the Youth League, the Trade Union, the Women's Federation and the Family Planning Commission. The Centre will convene an annual network meeting in order to receive feedback from information users and to make plans for future cooperation. The Centre will act as a matchmaker to bring people together. We will come to have a more central role. In this way, the Centre can survive. The aim is to support the building of local practice. Thus, if a network of many social workers and professionals from the Women's Federation, the Family Planning Commission, the Education Commission and the Trade Union can work together and identify the same ideas and concepts, then it will be easier to influence the government. Slowly the government can change its thinking to include new topics in the school curriculum.

Children do not only need to learn maths and geography. They also need knowledge about themselves – about their biology and their sexual development. There can be lots of questions and problems with regard to sexual intercourse or abortion. Our aim is to gradually include these topics in the formal curriculum. Previously the Family Planning Commission did not provide any service whatsoever to unmarried people. Previously, their attitude was that 'these are just children and we don't have to concern ourselves with them'. They now recognize that there are problems, so they have started to sign contracts with schools to carry out adolescent education. The local government has to decide to include sexual education in the curriculum. Gradually there will be a change at all levels that has been effectuated from below. I don't think that an NGO can influence the central government. We can only influence the very small local level government and then, gradually, change will take place up-wards through the system – from the district government to the city government to the provincial level and so on. And we have already influenced them, as in the following example of the Dongcheng District in Beijing.

The Dongcheng District decided to provide sexual education to adolescents, so they set up a Population School and they invited the JFC to give talks about sexology to adolescents and their parents. The State Family Planning Commission then sent two vice-presidents to have a meeting with representatives from the Dongcheng District population school and representatives of the JFC and to listen to our experience. Last summer [1997] a meeting was held in Dongcheng District to spread our experience and knowledge to Family Planning Commissions in all the other Beijing districts, so now Xicheng and Fengtai Districts both want to cooperate with the JFC. However, this year [1998] we are not engaging in any activities – we don't have any funds and they don't have any either – so we will do this next year. In this way our influence is relatively extensive.

When we visited Sweden we also invited the State Education Commission and the Family Planning Commission to come along. The Swedish Development Agency (Sida) had invited a delegation to visit Sweden to learn about sex education and to visit youth centres. We invited the director of the Beijing Family Planning Commission and the president of the Education Department of the State Family Planning Commission. The aim was to let them join us and see how NGOs can function and how sex education should be introduced into family planning education. They were very active when they returned. The State Family Planning Commission invited three JFC experts to give lectures to their headquarter staff in order to influence their headquarters. When they organized a group of experts to go to Zhejiang they also invited the JFC. So I feel that this reflects that the JFC has considerable influence.

Another sphere of influence concerns social work. In the past China did not have social work and social welfare. In the present times, with their focus on economic development, there is very little focus on social issues. The focus is on unemployment issues and other matters directly related to economic progress. In May [1998] we held a meeting with the national level Trade Union to discuss the relationship between unemployment and family and marriage problems such as domestic violence. We have seen many examples of laid-off women workers who have no income. They feel terrible and their husbands discriminate against them and treat them badly. Thus, we have been looking at the relationship between unemployment and marriage and family problems. If the husband and wife have a good relationship they can support each other through times of crisis, no matter which of them is unemployed. But if they fight with each other and one of them loses their job, the situation is much worse.

Another problem is single mothers who lose their jobs and do not have money to support their children. Now the Department of Women Workers of the Beijing Trade Union, following the suggestion of the JFC, has carried out a survey of single mothers who have lost their jobs to investigate their difficulties. The JFC has suggested that there should be a special social welfare policy for single parents – especially single women. Following the big Conference on Family, Social Welfare and Social Security in [1998] we held a smaller meeting to discuss the fact that social security policy does not include any special support for unemployed single parents, despite the fact that many and most of these are single mothers. We have suggested that there should be a special social security policy. We needed an investigation to illustrate that there is a need for special support, so the JFC suggested to the Department of Women Workers that they should carry out an investigation, and they agreed that this was very important. Their recent survey shows that laid off women workers who are also divorced and have children under the age of 18 have the most difficult situation. This is just the result of a small part of the investigation, which is still being conducted. We will analyse the findings together with them. If the JFC had not pointed out the special problems of divorced mothers, they would probably not have carried out this investigation. They do general surveys on unemployed women. We pointed to divorce as a relevant variable to be aware of and they realised that this was important. Furthermore, the small-scale investigation that they have already carried out demonstrates that this group of women has special difficulties. The JFC does not have a large enough budget to carry out a survey on its own, but it will write a report based on the survey data together with the Department of Women Workers, and that report will be delivered to the highest levels of the All China Federation of Trade Unions Welfare Department. If the Trade Union is willing to set up a special fund aimed at supporting single unemployed mothers, it will have to be approved by the central government. In this process the situation of single unemployed women will be revealed to the central government and the People's Congress. In this manner, we generate influence from below.

The JFC does not have any channels through which to influence the People's Congress and Central Government directly, but we are continuously struggling to find such channels. Recently we acquired a new channel of influence. The Democratic League has a Department of Women and I have become deputy director, so now I am in the position to write proposals directly to the People's Political Consultative Conference and the Peoples Congress. This year [1998] I will possibly write a proposal concerning the difficulties of single mothers. Previously, they thought that economic development concerns economics alone and they would therefore not look at social issues. But many non-economic factors do in fact influence economic development, so our aim is to make them realise how youth issues, women's issues and men's issues all affect the overall social and economic development.

4 The Migrant Women's Club

The greatest problem in China is that half the population is excluded from development, and that planning does not take into consideration that women are human beings. This is why gender awareness is necessary. (Wu Qing, speech at *Rural Women Knowing All* meeting, 26 July 1997)

The Migrant Women's Club held its inaugural meeting amid wide media attention in April 1996.[1] The organization was set up by *Rural Women Knowing All* (*Nongjianü baishitong*) – the first magazine to be published for rural women in China – and is one of several activities carried out under the auspices of the magazine. Other activities include providing literacy training for women in rural villages, the establishment of a development fund for rural women,[2] a rural women's reproductive health programme, and an investigation on

1. The following media wrote about the event: *Beijing wanbao* [Beijing Evening News] 13 April 1996, *Beijing qingnianbao* [Beijing Youth Daily] 8 April 1996, *Fazhi ribao* [Legal Daily] 19 April 1996, *Nongmin ribao* [Farmer's Daily] 9 April 1996, *Shenghuo shibao* [Life Times] 9 April 1996, *Renmin ribao* [People's Daily, overseas edition] 23 April 1996, *Weinin fuwu* [Service Weekly] 11 April 1996 and *Xinhua dianxun* [Xinhua Daily Telegraph] 23 April 1996.
2. The Chinese Rural Women's Education and Development Fund was set up by Wu Qing and Xie Lihua, who were inspired by the Grameen Bank. The fund was initially based on a donation from the author Bing Xin. By 2000 the magazine was engaged in three main projects: the Migrant Women's Club, a Practical Skills Training Centre for Rural Women and a Micro-credit Project.

suicide among rural women based on information gathered from letters sent to the magazine. From August 1995, following the success of a six-month series on rural migrants, *Rural Women Knowing All* featured several pages on rural migrant women in each issue under the heading 'Living Away From Home'. The overwhelming number of responses from migrant readers to the attention that was being given to their particular predicament led to the idea of setting up an organization especially for these young women. The aim was to support them by providing advice and service that would help them overcome the problems confronting them in the urban environment. Migration to urban China is a phenomenon related to the economic reforms, since restrictions on temporary migration have been significantly relaxed since 1978, allowing for individual or family-motivated migration to supplement the previous forms, which were mainly state-initiated (Davin 1999, Mallee and Pieke 1999). A host of new employment opportunities have been provided for a rural population whose labour, for more than two decades, had been underemployed and under-utilized; and it is estimated that between 40 and 100 million rural inhabitants had migrated to urban areas by the mid-1990s (Solinger 1998). An estimated three million people, of which about one third were women, migrated to Beijing.[3] In a study of female peasant-workers in the special economic zone Shenzhen in south China, Pun Ngai has argued that new social identities are created for rural migrant women, portraying them as inferior. Divisions between rural and urban, male and female, and different parts of China are all manipulated to maintain and extend new forms of domination and hierarchy (Pun Ngai 1999).

The term *dagongmei* in the Chinese name of the Club – *Dagongmei zhi jia* – gained popularity from the mid-1980s as the number of rural to urban migrants increased:

> *Dagongmei* is a newly coined term, denoting a new kind of labour relationship fundamentally different from those of Mao's period. A Cantonese term imported from Hong Kong, its meanings are multi-layered. *Dagong* means 'working for the boss', or 'selling labour', connoting commodification and a capitalist exchange of labour for wages. *Mei* means younger sister. It denotes not merely gender, but also marital status – *mei* is single, unmarried and younger (and thus

---

3. Several studies have indicated that in general more men than women migrate. According to two 1994 surveys the ratio of men to women leaving rural areas was 4.49:1 and 2.58:1 respectively (quoted in Tan 1995: 163 and 170).

of lower status). In contrast to the term 'worker' (*gongren*), which carried the highest status in the socialist rhetoric of Mao's day, the new word *dagong* signifies a lesser identity – that of hired hand – in a new context shaped by the rise of market factors in labour relations and hierarchy. (Pun Ngai 1999: 2)

The word *jia* in the club name means home. As a contrast to the various forms of discrimination experienced by rural women in the unfamiliar urban setting, it is the aim of the Migrant Women's Club to offer a place where they can feel at home, say what is on their minds without reservation and express heartfelt wishes; a place where they do not feel inferior and lonely. The organization describes itself as 'a warm place to go where there is no discrimination, no cold indifference and no inequality.' It is a place where 'everyone can speak as much as they like without inhibition' and where rural women can mutually support each other and find friends ('Dagong mei zhi jia' bangongshi 1996). My visits to the Club in 1996 and 1997 confirmed that members who took part in club activities seemed to be relaxed and at home. The number of members who telephoned or came to the office during the week to talk or to seek advice also gave evidence that members experienced the Club as a safe space where they could find help and support. In one case an unmarried member turned to the Club for help when she became pregnant, and in another case staff checked up and put pressure on the workplace of a member who was not receiving the training agreed upon in her work contract. In some cities migrant women are gathered into informal networks based on their place of origin to facilitate exchange of experiences and mutual assistance with the aim of improving living and working conditions and wages (Solinger 1998: 27–29, Zhang Junzuo 1994: 88). The Migrant Women's Club, set up by magazine staff for rural migrants, is engaged in the more far-reaching objective of creating a change in urban–rural and gender hierarchies. The aim is to provide support to individual members, to facilitate mutual support among members and to go beyond individual members by focusing attention on their problems as general social problems. It is this aim which earns the organization its definition as a social movement organization. This chapter describes club activities and analyses these with a focus on the role they play in challenging dominant norms and practices in society related to migrant women.

The two main initiators of the Migrant Women's Club were the editor of *China Women's News*, Xie Lihua (who was also chief editor of *Rural Women Knowing All* when the Club was set up), and Professor

Figure 11: Xie Lihua (on left) with members of the Migrant Women's Club. (Photo: The Migrant Women's Club)

Wu Qing. Wu Qing is active in local politics and has been an elected people's deputy to the Haidian District People's Congress in Beijing Municipality since 1984 and to the Beijing Municipal People's Congress since 1987. Xie Lihua is director of the Club and Wu Qing is advisor to both the magazine and the Club.[4] Wu Qing is a member of the board of the Global Fund for Women, and based on her contacts with international women's organizations, she has been able to support several of the new popular organizations in securing funding from international donors. She sees herself as a bridge builder not only between China and other countries but also between rural and urban China.[5]

An organization within an organization – the organizational structure of the Club

On the administrative level, the magazine *Rural Women Knowing All*, published monthly since January 1993, is a sub-division of the news-

4. A *Rural Women Knowing All* article by Xie Lihua introduces Professor Wu Qing to readers. See Xie Lihua (1995b) 'Women de guwen – Wu Qing' [Our Advisor – Wu Qing]. *Rural Women Knowing All*, No. 8, pp. 4–6.
5. See Bode 1995 for an interview by Isabel Crook, Liu Dongxiao and Lisa Stearns with Wu Qing about her political activism.

paper *Zhongguo funübao* [*China Women's News*], which has in turn been published by the All China Women's Federation since 1984. Among some 10,000 newspapers and magazines published in China, including about 50 published by the ACWF, there was none specifically intended for a rural female readership although the great majority of women in China are from rural areas (Xie 1995c: 222). The magazine was an initiative of the ACWF, which obtained a permit from the State Circulation and Publication Bureau to publish a textbook like magazine targeting rural women (Liu Dongxiao 1999: 5). However, according to Wu Qing:

> Nobody would take on the task of creating a magazine for country bumpkins, as well as the double handicap of dealing with something concerning both *rural* and *women*. No one dared. People are afraid of losing money ... Xie Lihua had the guts to do it. She has had opportunities to go to rural areas, so she knew the needs and demands and the market. (Wu Qing, interview 1997)

Xie Lihua explains that in her work at *China Women's News* she already had experience in combining journalism with social activities, in the sense that her writing and editing had been extended to activism to improve women's lives. When she took on the job of editing *Rural Women Knowing All* Xie Lihua chose to combine journalism with activism:[6]

> Our thinking is NGO thinking. The Women's Federation has a government background, but is really also a mass organization, so I feel that linking up to the ACWF is good ... Nobody asked us to set up the Club, but we believe it is beneficial to women, so in this sense I need to depend on the Federation to carry out activities. Our possibilities for reaching out to women, especially rural women, are limited. I feel that because I am part of the Federation I am trusted, but I am also a journalist and some of my thinking is also non-governmental thinking. So I think linking up to the Federation is an advantage. This makes work so much easier than it is for Wang Xingjuan and Chen Yiyun. Wang Xingjuan's work has extensive social impact, but if she wants to do something practical it is difficult. I am employed by the Federation and have its network to draw upon. Chen Yiyun has linked up with the Trade Union because she mainly works with urban women. It is a special characteristic of China that you need to depend on some institution. (Xie Lihua, interview 1997)

---

6. For an account of Xie Lihua's activism, see Mufson 1998.

The rationale and implications of linking up to party-state institutions will be elaborated in Chapter Five. In practical organizational terms, when the magazine was set up *China Women's News* granted Xie Lihua paid leave of absence, supported the new magazine financially and provided office space. Until June 1997, when *China Women's News* and the magazine moved to new premises, the Migrant Women's Club office was situated in a small office leading into the main magazine office, thus enabling close contact between Club and magazine staff. When the magazine moved, the Club stayed in the old building. Both the magazine and Club are able to use the extensive ACWF nationwide administrative system. Campaigns to secure subscriptions have, for example, been carried out in cooperation with local-level Women's Federations. Funding of activities has continuously been a major problem for popular organizations such as the Women's Research Institute/Maple Women's Psychological Counselling Centre and the Jinglun Family Centre, which are largely dependent on funding from non-Chinese donor organizations. The Migrant Women's Club has received non-Chinese donor funding, just as these organizations have. Because the work of both the magazine and the Club targets rural women, links to local branches of the ACWF are essential to successful implementation of the activities that take place in rural areas. The Club has, for example, provided micro credit loans to women for the establishment of agricultural production or businesses (for instance animal husbandry, a shop or a restaurant) when they leave Beijing. Not only do women need funding to establish a business; they also need the support of the local Women's Federation and of local authorities to acquire the necessary permits and registrations. In this context, *Rural Women Knowing All* provides a means of reaching out to local Women's Federation branches and informing them of the needs of returning migrants in order to enlist their support for these women. In February 1996, journalist Li Tao accompanied club member Wang Dingbi, who had then worked in Beijing for six years, on her first visit back to her village in Sichuan province. The immediate purpose of the visit was to investigate possibilities for one individual club member to realize plans for opening a kindergarten in the village upon her return (Wang Dingbi 1997, Li Tao 1997). The wider social movement aim – or, to use Molyneux's (1985) concept, the strategic gender interest – of the visit and the coverage in the magazine was to create an image of the migrant woman as a full-scale, equal citizen by providing an example of a migrant woman returning to her place of origin and – using the skills she had acquired in the city – to contribute to the development of her home community.

Club members

In terms of recruitment methods and the relationship between the organization and its constituency, the Migrant Women's Club is an innovative type of membership organization within the People's Republic of China. Membership of the Women's Federation is, in principle, automatic for all women in China. Similarly, the professional women's organizations that have been established since the 1980s have more or less automatically included all women within a specific profession as their members. Contrary to this form of automatic membership, the Migrant Women's Club recruited its first members in March 1996 by issuing 2,000 letters to hospitals and factories employing rural women and to eight service enterprises that facilitate contact between rural migrants and urban employers in Beijing. Subsequently, about two hundred women registered as members. They did so by obtaining and filling in a membership application form at the Migrant Women's Club office and paying a membership fee of three yuan.[7] In December 1996, 196 young women who had migrated to Beijing from rural areas were registered as members of the Migrant Women's Club.[8] The average age of the members was 21.5 years, the eldest being 36 and the youngest 16. Most had been in Beijing for more than three years at the time they became members. The majority were engaged in various forms of unskilled labour as maids in private homes, factory workers, waitresses in restaurants and shop assistants. Only a few were engaged in skilled labour, for example as typists and accountants (Li Tao 1996: 17).[9]

Staff and organizers

The Migrant Women's Club is staffed both by people different from those whom the organization serves and by a few rural migrant

---

7. Requirements for becoming a member were registration with the relevant migration authorities and possession of a temporary residence permit in Beijing.

8. Their provinces of origin were: Shandong 75, Sichuan 52, Hebei 26, Henan 22, Anhui 5, Shanxi 3, Gansu 3, while 10 came from other provinces (Li Tao 1996).

9. According to one 1995 *Rural Women Knowing All* article, approximately half of all rural women working in the city work as helpers (*banggongnü*) and many are engaged in the lowest paid and dirtiest work preparing food, cleaning and serving in restaurants (Zhao Shilin 1995).

women. In discussing the relationship between an organization and the constituency that it represents, Farrington *et al.* (1993: 3) distinguish between organizations staffed by the people they are meant to serve and represent and organizations staffed by people who are different (socially, professionally, ethnically) from their members. The two types of organizations have different relationships with their constituencies in terms of member participation in defining needs and determining the activities of the organization – organizations staffed by members of the constituency represent the more participatory approach. During the first fifteen months, the core staff and organizers consisted of Xie Lihua, journalist Li Tao of *Rural Women Knowing All*, and Yu Jinglian and Zhang Xin as office staff. Li Tao is himself a migrant from Shandong province, who spent many years of his childhood and youth in a rural village and is thus familiar with the circumstances from which club members come. Following her retirement, Yu Jinglian worked as a volunteer at the Women's Research Institute office for several years before she started work at the Migrant Women's Club in June 1996. Zhang Xin, a young rural woman from Shandong province, worked as a maid before joining the staff of *Rural Women Knowing All* and Migrant Women's Club. Considering the fact that rural migrants generally are ostracized by the urban population, choosing to engage a migrant woman as one of two office staff members is a significant step. It reflects recognition on the part of the organizers that they do not share the members' experience of being rural migrants, and that they are in fact attempting to include them and base their work on their needs. Working in close cooperation with this core staff group are a number of volunteer activists as well as staff from the Beida Hospital, where about half of the Migrant Women's Club members work.

It is an important stated objective of the organization to base its work on the needs and interests of its members as well as on their active participation in planning club activities to suit these. One of the reasons for setting up a special organization for rural migrant women mentioned by *Rural Women Knowing All* journalist Li Tao in an article on the history and activities of the Migrant Women's Club is that the available training courses for rural women viewed the women as 'passive receivers of training' and did not base training on their needs (Li Tao 1996: 14). Although the Migrant Women's Club during the time of this study (the first fifteen months of its existence) did not have a formal structure to ensure the active participation of members in setting the agenda of the Club, a meeting held in March

Figure 12: Zhang Xin with Club members at a Sunday meeting in July 1998. (Photo: Cecilia Milwertz)

Figure 13: Zhang Xin and Yu Jinglian at the Club office in 1998. (Photo: Cecilia Milwertz)

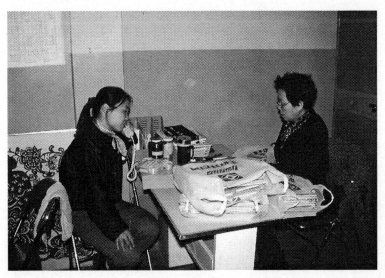

1997 to plan the Club's activities for the coming three month period illustrated how members were included in the planning and decision making process. Present at the meeting were six club members and the core staff: Xie Lihua, Yu Jinglian, Zhang Xin and Li Tao. Also attending the meeting were Dai Dongying from the magazine office, two representatives from the Department of Temporary Workers at Beida Hospital, a representative from a service enterprise for rural women in the East District of Beijing, which also cooperates with the Club, and volunteer activist Wen Huaping. While the members were not the main actors or decision makers at the meeting, their voices were heard as they participated in planning future club activities. These included the one-year anniversary celebration, a collective wedding ceremony where five couples were to be married, a language competition, a talk on Hong Kong and a visit to a village on the outskirts of Beijing.

Issues addressed by the Club

The two fundamental issues addressed by the Migrant Women's Club are the social and economic gap between urban and rural China and gender inequality. As described by the Club, migrants from rural to urban areas come to personify the gap between rural, agricultural and urban, industrialized life-styles. Rural women in the city are discriminated against in terms of working conditions, they find their knowledge and skills inadequate for coping with urban life and they have problems due to their rural household registration. Club members have been shocked to find that not only do employers take advantage of them, but that the urban population seems to be generally hostile towards them (Li Tao 1996: 9–10). In a letter to the magazine, one woman wrote that she felt extremely humiliated when she first met her potential employer, who looked at her not as a fellow human being, but 'at best as if she were buying a high-quality commodity'. (Xie Lihua 1995a: 6). Much of the discrimination experienced by rural migrants is not gender-specific. However, according to the Club initiators, rural women migrants are particularly exposed and vulnerable in the urban context. Their decision to work for the cause of rural women is based on their view that if China in general, despite the great progress attained under Communist Party rule, has a long way to go in achieving gender equality within a cultural context in which women are viewed as 'second class citizens', then rural women are those that are most disadvantaged (Xie Lihua and Wu Qing, interview 1997). All members of the Migrant Women's Club have experienced discrimination at the hands of urban citizens. Not only do the women serve as cheap labour in the cities, taking on work that urban citizens themselves are unwilling to do; they also receive the lowest pay, their social status is low, their lifestyle is perceived as backward and their educational level is inadequate. All in all, there is an immense difference between urban and rural life-styles, leading to prejudice and pressure from the host population, which in turn make the migrant women feel inferior.

A number of surveys and studies provide an overall picture of the extent of the problems. These include long working hours, poor working and living conditions, lack of labour contracts and social security measures, physical and verbal abuse, sexual harassment and rape (Davin 1999, Tan 1995, Solinger 1998, Tang Can 1996). Letters and articles published in *Rural Women Knowing All* provide examples of the problems confronting rural migrants. In one letter published in the magazine, Wang Haiying, a 22-year-old woman who migrated from her village of origin when she was 17, writes about how difficult it was for her to be admitted to hospital in Guangzhou when she became ill while working at a factory there.[10] When one hospital finally did admit her, she had nothing to eat for four days because she had no money.[11] Furthermore, because she was ill, she lost her job. She later worked for four years in Beijing as a maid for a family who paid her very little (Wang Haiying 1995). Another young woman writes of how she worked at a Beijing restaurant for a miserable salary. The board and lodgings included in her wages turned out to be a bed made only of wooden boards and meals consisting mostly of leftovers from the tables she served (Hongjie 1995).[12] To inform rural women of their legal rights, work on compiling a 'Manual for Migrant Girls' was started in 1997. Based on a series of case studies, the idea was to translate laws and regulations relevant to the lives of rural migrants into language comprehensible to them, and to provide them with information on the relevant authorities and

---

10. According to the household registration system, legal matters can only be resolved at the place of registration and only authorities at the place of registration are responsible for citizens. This means for instance that a hospital is not obliged to admit someone who is registered in another part of China.

11. As a rule, a patient's family must bring food in for him/her during a hospital stay.

12. However, Hongjie's story, like several others, does have a happy ending when she realizes the dream of opening her own restaurant.

institutions to contact when in need of support. Often, rural women are not aware that they have legal rights in the labour market and that these are being violated. And even if they are aware that their rights are being violated, they do not necessarily know where to seek assistance. The Club has cooperated with the Centre for Women's Law Studies and Legal Services, which has taken up cases of club members, and whose lawyers have given talks at the Club. Although the Club, in cooperation with *Rural Women Knowing All*, has been involved in solving specific problems encountered by members, it does not have the capacity to resolve conflicts by providing social service and legal aid on a larger scale. When members seek support to solve problems related to their employment or other matters, the role of the Club is, in principle, mainly to provide information, moral support and guidance, and to facilitate contact to the ACWF and employment authorities that can deal specifically with the problems.

However, it was precisely the encounter with individual women and their problems that led the magazine staff to comprehend the extent of discrimination against rural migrant women and their need for support. In one example, the staff of *Rural Women Knowing All* helped Chen Cundi, who later became a Migrant Women's Club member, to obtain a divorce from the husband to whom she had been sold. This took place before the establishment of the Club. Chen Cundi had been abducted by a woman who had offered her a job in another province. When she arrived there, she discovered that she had been sold into marriage. Although she managed to escape from her husband, five years passed before Chen Cundi reached Beijing, where she came into contact with the magazine staff. A journalist and a lawyer travelled with her to both her own and her husband's provinces, where they assisted her in contacting the relevant Women's Federation and legal authorities in order to obtain a divorce. Because her husband had paid her mother a large sum of money, Chen Cundi did not believe that she had the right to leave him or to obtain a divorce.[13] Following the divorce, Chen Cundi said that she would have stayed with her husband had it not been for the fact that he was beating her. In 1997 she explained:

> He had a very bad temper. He often abused and hit me. So I did not stay for more than a couple of months. He would lock the door

---

13. The amount he had paid was 6,000 yuan, at a time when a monthly urban salary for a rural migrant was about 200 yuan.

when he left for work. I tried to run away and he beat me. My brother tried to help me but then he beat my brother. Finally, my brother helped me to run away across the fields. I wanted to end the marriage, but I did not dare. Without my consent, I had been married and my household registration had been moved to my husband's province. Thus, the authorities in Shaanxi province would not help me, as I was now registered in Hebei province. And as long as I was married, I could not move my registration. My husband said I could get a divorce if I repaid him all the money he had spent to buy me. I felt just like an egg hitting against a stone. My mother wanted me to return to my husband. She is a very typical Chinese rural woman. (Chen Cundi, interview 1997)

Chen Cundi had been taken in by deceit and sold at a time when her family was desperately poor. Her father had just died at the age of fifty, due to the family's lack of funds for medical care. She considered committing suicide, but finally managed to flee. Contact with magazine staff and membership in the Club meant an enormous change for her. By early 1997, she was part of a group of three club members who gave talks in Beijing to recruit new members. Previously, she said, she would never have dared to stand up and speak in front of many people. In fact, she hardly dared approach the Club to join it. She said felt inferior, as she was 'only a maid'. It is unlikely that she, even in her wildest dreams, would have imagined that she could actually end the marriage into which she had been sold, not least because divorce initiated by the woman does not accord with the prevalent cultural assumptions about gender relations. When she left her husband and returned to her home village, Chen Cundi was looked down upon by fellow villagers because she was not complying with her role as a married woman by accepting her destiny (Chen Cundi, interview 1997).

The approach applied by the Club in supporting rural women migrants is based on the fact that equality between men and women is officially guaranteed by Chinese law. However, the Club views insufficient labour market legislation as one of the reasons that rural migrant women are discriminated against and emphasizes the importance of improving legislation in this area. Under the present circumstances, the aim is primarily to rectify the imbalance between the legal and proclaimed equality on the one hand and the actual discrimination in daily life on the other by ensuring that women know their rights and by creating a general awareness in society of the rights and situation of rural migrant women. The Club's objective is both to provide members with knowledge of their legal rights and to unite rural women and their urban employers in breaching the urban–rural gap. In aiming to improve the relationship between migrant and host populations, the Club is engaged in a delicate balancing act between supporting rural migrant women and simultaneously convincing employers that in the long run this is not contrary to their interests.

Members of the Club, like the majority of migrants in China, fall into the category of what is termed the 'floating' population. This means that their residence in the city is temporary, and that they are permanently registered in their rural place of origin. Many migrants will leave the city at some point, either by choice or because they cannot gain permanent residence there. All citizens in China are registered at birth as either urban or rural residents. Apart from temporary urban residence permits, it is extremely difficult to change a rural status to an urban one. Originally, this registration system was set up in order to limit migration from the countryside to the cities. According to Xie Lihua, the Club does not encourage members to return to rural areas, but plays a role in supporting them so that they can cope, if and when they choose or are compelled to return. Conversations with club members give the impression that while some members have been sent to the city to earn money to support their families, and plan only to stay in the city as long as their families require them to do so, others are set on avoiding return. In mid-1997 Xie Lihua discovered that a group of twenty rural migrant women in Xiamen, a South China coastal city, had been granted urban residence permits in recognition of the contribution that rural migrants were making to the development of the city. The Migrant Women's Club invited these women to visit Beijing for a meeting with the dual objectives of morally supporting club members' wishes to remain in the city and staging a media event to promote a change of attitudes towards granting urban residence to rural women migrants – especially those who marry urban residents. In order to prevent rural to urban migration, the household registration system registers children according to their mothers' place of origin; consequently, children of a rural mother living in the city cannot, even if their father holds an urban household permit, receive urban schooling (Davin 1999: 6). Xie Lihua's view is that

> [i]t is important to solve the household registration issue for migrants. In its present form the system is harmful to women. Some places now permit the child to follow the registration of the father or the mother. This benefits the education of the children and corresponds

to changes in society. Even though the problem has only been resolved for twenty women, I consider this as progress. Media publicity of the case of these twenty women will cause government officials to start thinking about the issue. (Xie Lihua, interview 1998)

The main objective of the Migrant Women's Club is to provide service to their members in the form of education 'according to their expressed needs' ('Dagong mei zhi jia' bangongshi 1996) in order to help them to solve the problems confronting them in the urban environment as well as in relation to their return to rural areas. The Club plays an important role in facilitating group support and letting women know that they are not alone: other women are in the same situation as they are and have similar problems. Having brought women together in the Club to share their experiences, the next aim is to support them in creating changes to improve their lives. They work to help members to recognize precisely where their problems and weaknesses lie, and to support them in confronting these, both as structurally imposed gender roles and urban/rural hierarchies, and when they stem from a lack of education and skills. The Club also aims to support migrant women in recognizing their own strengths in situations in which they are constantly being told that they lack 'quality' (*suzhi*).[14] According to Club initiators Xie Lihua and Wu Qing, members receive guidance in changing their way of thinking, and the Club aims to offer them alternatives.

The types of activities aimed at fulfilling these member-related objectives of the Club during the first fifteen months after the establishment of the organization were mainly lectures, basic education and excursions. At some meetings, experts were asked to give a talk, while at other meetings, speakers were rural women who talked from personal experience. At one such meeting held in May 1996, Zhang Huanrong, a successful 28-year-old poultry breeder, had been invited to talk about her experience in setting up the enterprise. At that time, she had 34 workers employed. Following Zhang Huanrongs's speech, Xie Lihua reminded the 50-odd members of the Migrant Women's Club who were in attendance that, due to the household registration system, they would have to leave Beijing at some point. 'Therefore', she said, 'it is important that each one decides what she wants to do and prepares herself for her future'. Xie Lihua stressed that Zhang Huanrong's story could provide support and strength for

---

14. For excerpts of a discussion of the issue of the 'quality' of women, see Hsiung, Jaschok and Milwertz (2001).

others by illustrating that even when there seems to be no way out one must believe in oneself. 'It does not help to think that because you are a woman you have to rely on others', she said. 'Everyone must rely on herself, and if you believe in yourself you can find the strength to overcome difficulties'. Thus, the purpose of the meeting was twofold. It was meant to prepare the women for their departure from the city in both a practical and a psychological sense. The problems that the women foresaw were reflected in the questions they asked. These basically revolved around two issues. First, questions concerning the relationship between Zhang Huanrong and her husband and parents-in-law reflected members' anticipation that rural areas would lack acceptance for a woman starting up her own enterprise. Second, there were questions related to specific practical issues in terms of the skills necessary for breeding poultry as well as in terms of funding and managing an enterprise.

Primary school and skills training

From December 1996, the Migrant Women's Club offered primary school classes in mathematics, Chinese and English to members who wanted to improve their basic education. The majority (86 per cent) of the 196 members registered in December 1996 had attended only six years of school (Li Tao 1996: 17). The teachers were themselves rural migrants. Journalist Li Tao taught the Chinese class, Zhang Xin from the Club office, who herself had graduated from upper middle school, taught mathematics, and English was taught by a club member who had graduated from a teachers' college. According to Zhang Xin, who was also coordinator of the classes, many of the women found the English class too difficult, but most have kept up the Chinese class. Chinese class participants found the classes useful because the lowest level otherwise taught for adults is usually upper middle school. Furthermore, they appreciated being taught by someone who did not make them feel inferior and stupid (interview with class participants April 1997). In 1997 a new book for the continuation of the Chinese class was being compiled by Zhang Xin. The idea was to collect a series of texts relevant to the lives of the students themselves. Plans were also under way to start classes in sewing, typing and computer skills as well as technical agricultural skills. The aim was to offer some of these classes in cooperation with an organization which was being set up under the auspices of China Women's News to train unemployed women. The purpose of this training is not only for rural women to acquire new

Figure 14: *Rural Women Knowing All* journalist Li Tao teaching a Chinese language class in 1998. (Photo: Cecilia Milwertz)

skills which will enable them to gain employment in the city or in rural areas, but also to help them overcome their feelings of inferiority, so that they will perceive of themselves as equals to urban citizens. In fact, the most obvious change in rural women who become members of the Club is, according to professor Wu Qing, that they acquire a greater sense of self-confidence.

Linking up with the media

In addition to ongoing educational activities and regular meetings, the Club organizes special activities such as anniversary celebrations. In 1997, a collective marriage ceremony was also held. By creating such events and making use of the interest of the media, the Club is able to reach a broad audience beyond its members. The main aim is to create a change of attitude among the urban populace towards rural migrants by presenting an alternative image of the migrants. Instead of exaggerating their numbers and stressing their most visible negative aspects, an alternative, positive image of migrants engaged in constructive activities is presented. The first anniversary celebration had several aims: first, it was an occasion on which members and staff of the Club could celebrate their achievements together; second, it was an opportunity to invite donor organization

Figure 15: Xie Lihua with Club members and their husbands at the collective marriage ceremony in 1997. (Photo: The Migrant Women's Club)

representatives to a presentation of these achievements; third, it was, via media coverage, a way of conveying a positive image of migrant women to the general public, and of pointing out their problems to the authorities. The celebration included singing, talks by club initiators, staff and supporters of the Club, and members' heartbreaking accounts of their individual life stories. The celebration was held in a large hall. At one end a long table for the main speakers was set up with rows of chairs for members and other participants facing this panel. Between the panel and the rows of participants was a space filled by TV reporters and their equipment. The result was that the massive number of media representatives separated participants from the panel, so that the some 200 club members and their supporters became not only participants in the celebration but also spectators at a media event. This was apparent in the function that the sharing of life stories took on at the event. Within the context of the Club itself, at Sunday meetings, when stories are shared among members, the recognition that their problems are not individual, but are actually reflections of broader issues in society, serves as the basis for change. In the context of the celebration, these same stories served the purpose of illustrating the great difficulties faced by migrant women. Storytelling in this situation served to create an image of this group of rural migrants as honest, hardworking contributors to the construction of the modern city.

The Club can only help a relatively small number of members to receive basic and legal education and to develop group support and mutual aid. However, the message that women can question unequal gender relations, put forward demands on the basis of their own definition of their interests and create change is being spread to a much larger number of women via the magazine. Furthermore, the population in general as well as the authorities are being influenced through the media to change their attitudes towards rural migrants. The link between the magazine and Club is not only structural, but is functionally incorporated into club activities. The case of Chen Cundi illustrates a Club practice of addressing a specific immediate problem, providing information and practical support to an individual and then going beyond the immediate practical gender interests of one migrant woman in order to challenge women's subordination in general. The Club extends its feminist activism beyond its few hundred members. When the Club and magazine help individual women to solve specific problems, the cases are covered in the magazine in order to create (gender) awareness about a general problem and to illustrate that alternative patterns of action are possible. Xie Lihua defines the link between the activities of the Club and media coverage in *Rural Women Knowing All* and *China Women's News* as essential to the objective of creating awareness in rural China in the sense that

> ... only the media can convey an understanding of the outside world, and only if there exists an alternative can the wish and impetus to change backward features arise. (Xie Lihua 1995c: 226)

Via its link to *Rural Women Knowing All*, which in 1997 had reached a distribution of 230,000, the Migrant Women's Club has been able to spread its message in support of creating gender equality and social justice, not only to the relatively small group of members, but to a larger group of rural women in both rural and urban China. The Club also engages the urban media in an effort to change the stereotypically negative image of the cheating, criminal migrant. Television, radio and other media regularly publicize activities of the Club such as the first anniversary. Commenting on the importance of presenting social issues from an alternative perspective, Xie Lihua says:

> We cannot know to what degree we have been successful in changing attitudes, but I do have examples of journalists who have changed the perspective of their articles on the migrant population once they

came to know the Club and its activities. Some people say I am just publicizing my own work. I do not agree. I am publicizing a belief and a way of working that represents a trend of development in society, so I really find that media publicity is very important. We bring forward social problems that deserve reflection. (Xie Lihua, interview 1998)

By representing the strategic interests of rural migrant women, the Club is, as discussed by Martha Nussbaum (1995) in the context of women's projects in India, imposing the values of an urban, intellectual women's movement upon women who otherwise have perceived of their own second-class status as 'right' and 'natural'. They assume that these women, although they do not necessarily articulate it, actually need and value autonomy. Provision of practical assistance by the Club to individual women is based on the immediate, practical needs of the women. Strategic gender interests are also 'imposed' to help the individual and as part of advocacy work. The Migrant Women's Club bases its work on the needs and interests as well as on the active participation of rural migrant women, at the same time that it 'imposes' strategic gender interests on them. It does so by challenging the sexual division of labour, and the traditional attitudes towards monetary loans to women, by challenging traditional beliefs about women's dependency on men and also traditional ideas that do not regard women as human beings. It also does so by promoting women's knowledge of their legal rights and insisting that women must acquire skills and be eco-nomically independent. Basically, the work of the Migrant Women's Club challenges and opposes cultural traditions and teaches women not to accept a second-class status. The idea that Chen Cundi could divorce her husband without paying him back was 'imposed' on her by magazine staff intervention. Going one step further than the expressed practical gender needs of rural women, as in this case, the magazine and the Club represent strategic gender interests, because rights, privileges and gender relations that subordinate women – and that are often taken for granted in Chinese society – are challenged here. Although the following does not refer specifically to the Migrant Women's Club, I believe that the aims that Wu Qing expresses for a gender-sensitive development policy in China cover the initiators' intentions for the Club very well:

[T]he first thing we need is consciousness raising. If people, the decision makers, do not have gender awareness, women will always be treated as second-class citizens. Therefore, there will be double standards, there will be separate projects. But we know that *separate can never be equal.* It is vital to sensitize people in the media sector, who have great influence over the general public. It is vital to sensitize women to help them gain self-esteem and confidence, so that they will try to better themselves economically, socially and politically. Then they will definitely become first active participants, then agents and partners of projects. (Wu Qing 1999: 68–69)

5

Forming a Movement Wave

The Women's Research Institute/Maple Women's Psychological Counselling Centre, the Jinglun Family Centre and the Migrant Women's Club are three separate and distinct organizations. They are also joined together as actors in a social movement wave that carries emancipatory civil society in its values, beliefs and practices. This chapter analyses the process of popular women's organizing in Beijing in the 1980s and 90s, explicated mainly by these three organizations but also including other organizations, as one important aspect of the formation of a new wave of the Chinese women's movement.

The three organizations have both similarities and differences in terms of their formal registration, their internal set-up, the issues that they address, the activities in which they engage and their modes of action. The main features which link them as collaborative actors in forming a new wave of the Chinese women's movement are: first, their position as popular forms of organizing; second, their shared commitment to eliminating gender inequality by creating social change; and third, their innovative discourse on gender issues – hence these features are the focus of this chapter.

Issues and activities – new perspectives and knowledge

The three organizations are engaged in four main types of activities aimed at three main target groups. The activities are first, provision of practical services to individuals; second, working to change attitudes and practices in society in general; third, advocacy aimed at legislative, executive and policy-making levels of authorities; and fourth, research – the results of which are aimed at all three target groups, since this fourth activity is used in relation to all of the other three. The process of organizing has developed understandings and interpretations of gendered social problems, and each organization has gradually focused its activities on the areas in which it has best been able to operate and make an impact. This is especially the case for the Women's Research Institute/Maple Women's Psychological Counselling Centre and the Jinglun Family Centre. They had been functioning for ten and eight years respectively when the final interviews for this study took place in 1998, whereas the Migrant Women's Club had only existed for two years at that time, and had not yet refined and developed its work to the same degree as the other two organizations. A common characteristic of all three organizations is that they are built by and around charismatic leaders. The way each organization has developed is to a high degree a question of the leader's choices and strategies and is based on her personal networks and relations, both internally to the organization's activists and externally to party-state institutions.

℘ Activities and internal structure

First, a brief summary of the types of activities in which each of the organizations has engaged and how these are related to their internal set-up. The Women's Research Institute was originally set up in order to provide indirect help to women whose lives were negatively affected by the reforms. The institute attempted to do this by carrying out research on issues which the founding members viewed as insufficiently covered or totally ignored by the leadership and academia – although the new women's studies centres were also beginning to address these issues. The institute's proposition was that a prerequisite for the authorities to engage in action to resolve problems such as gender-based unemployment and prostitution was that these were thoroughly investigated and documented. Their aim was to undertake research and present the results to the authorities. Not until 1991, when first the Singles Weekend Club was established, and especially in 1992 (that is, three–four years following its establishment) with the first Women's Hotline, did the Women's Research Institute begin to provide direct practical assistance to individual women. Since then, research activities have been linked to the provision of services. Other hotlines have been established and together these hotlines have become the core activity of the Maple

Women's Psychological Counselling Centre. They provide services to individual women and data for research, and research results are used to lobby for policy and legal change. A relatively large number of activists engaged in providing practical services characterizes the internal organizational structure of the Women's Research Institute/ Maple Women's Psychological Counselling Centre. First the Institute, and later the Centre, have continuously engaged about 50 volunteer hotline counsellor activists. Some have provided counselling for nearly ten years since the inception of the first Women's Hotline in 1992. Others have left over the years, but new activists have been recruited to continue their work. The many activists who carry out the work of the Centre meet more or less regularly at monthly Hotline counselling meetings. A smaller number of these activists are also Hotline counselling supervisors and researchers who form a relatively stable core group of activists attached to the organization.

Establishment of the Jinglun Family Centre grew out of Chen Yiyun's research. Aware of the many reform-period problems relating especially to marriage and family issues, she wanted to go behind the statistics to study the living people who were being affected. Once she started interviewing workers, students, and intellectuals, she realized that there was a vast unmet need for counselling. Thus, the Jinglun Family Centre was initially engaged mainly in providing both telephone and face-to-face psychological counselling services directly from the Centre offices and via other institutions. In the early years telephone and face-to-face counselling was provided by the China Administration College for Women Cadres and the Girls' Classes and Girls' Club were delegated to the Youth College. As will be discussed in more detail below, on the one hand, a considerable strength of the Jinglun Family Centre's work has been the ability to work closely with several party-state institutions. On the other hand, the scattered locations of activists in many different institutions with relatively loose links to the Centre has meant that the Centre has not had a long-term core group of activists involved in day-to-day maintenance or planning future Centre activities. Together with Director Chen Yiyun, changing deputy directors and members of the Centre Council have been the most closely attached activists. The Jinglun Family Centre started out by providing direct counselling and other services to individuals, but has chosen more or less to discontinue these activities in order to focus entirely on education.

The Migrant Women's Club grew out of the magazine *Rural Women Knowing All.* Readers of both the magazine and the newspaper *China*

Women's News sent letters to the magazine describing their problems, and the staff, led by Xie Lihua, then decided to provide assistance to them. Since the Club was established, magazine staff have primarily been involved in covering Club events in the magazine. They have assisted actual Club-employed staff in organizing media-related events. The Club differs both from the Women's Research Institute and the Jinglun Family Centre in that it is a member organization. The activities of the Club are aimed at helping the members themselves. Club activities are also closely linked to the magazine and additional aims, based on the activities of the Club, are to assist the readership of the magazine, and to influence the general populace and the authorities.

Whether they started off by providing practical assistance to individual women or by engaging in research, the establishment of the three organizations was a reaction to problems faced especially by women, either as a direct consequence of economic reforms, or surfacing in connection with the reforms. The organizations were founded on the premise that equality between men and women was legally guaranteed in the Constitution, the Marriage Law and, since 1992, the Law on the Protection of the Rights and Interests of Women.[1] For all three organizations, activities have been aimed both at rectifying the imbalance between the legal and proclaimed equality and the actual discrimination against women in daily life, and at ensuring that women's rights are actually respected at all levels of society.

ℰℴ Transformation of knowledge

A central aim of the organizations is to change those attitudes and practices which hinder the development of gender equality by providing knowledge and information to the three target groups – individuals, the population in general and the authorities. Questioning and redefining knowledge – i.e. defining and documenting 'what is known in a particular field or in total' – is central to all types of activities: services, research and advocacy. This process challenges dominant discourses and established norms and practices, and promotes alternatives so as to change attitudes and practices and break taboos within fields to which little or no attention has previously been given. One of the first stages in this process is the realization that it is possible to question dominant discourses existing within the society.

---

1. For a list of laws and other 'important measures concerning women's rights in China since 1980', see Tan Lin and Peng Xizhi (2000): Table 12.3.

The experience of an activist who did not want to attend the 1995 Women's Conference NGO Forum illustrates how this realization can come about. A limited number of 5,000 Chinese participants was admitted to the NGO Forum. Many more wanted to take part. Yet, although a well-known media researcher was allocated a much sought-after spot, she was extremely reluctant to have anything whatsoever to do with the Forum. She had conducted a UNESCO-funded study of the role of women journalists in the Chinese media, and was appointed by her research institute to present the results at a Forum workshop. While she was quite happy to present her work, she envisioned the NGO Forum as a meeting of thousands of All China Women's Federation-type cadres from all over the world, and she had no wish whatsoever to be part of such an encounter. Her personal experience with workplace representatives of the Women's Federation was not good. While working at a factory in the 1970s, she was ordered, together with the other women, to wash the clothes of all their male co-workers on March 8 – International Women's Day. And she had refused to do so, since her understanding of equality between men and women was not exactly in accord with women sacrificing themselves and their holiday.

This was just one of many clashes between this researcher and the dominant gender discourse that she encountered in society and she experienced displacement or alienation in relation to the ACWF and its policies because her alternative discourse on women's liberation did not match the official party-state and ACWF discourse. However, as has been theorized by psychologist Jette Fog (1985), she did not have concepts with which to label her discourse, nor did she realize that alternative discourses beyond her own were possible. Being able to place a name on an alternative discourse – something she experienced when, in the end, she did take part in both the preparations for the NGO Forum and the Forum itself – provided the opportunity to transform her 'minority' identity into an oppositional one, and into activism. She was overwhelmed to find that her hitherto generally unaccepted identity and understanding of gender equality already had been identified and named by others. The story of this one activist provides more than anecdotal evidence, as the history of women's popular organizing in Beijing in the 1980s and 1990s is full of similar stories of how individual activists and groups have come together to become aware of and reinterpret patterns in women's lives. One activist from the East Meets West Group writes:

I came to acquire words and concepts such as gender discrimination, gender stereotype, gender roles and gendered structure. I began to put things in perspective, a gender perspective. I was amazed at the effectiveness and forcefulness of these English words in describing and deconstructing women's secondary position in families and societies. (Ge Youli, in Ge and Jolly 2001)

In their cognitive approach to studying social movements, sociologists Ron Eyerman and Andrew Jamison have defined this transformation of knowledge experienced by activists as 'a cognitive territory' and as 'new conceptual space that is filled by a dynamic interaction between different groups and organisations' (Eyerman and Jamison 1991: 55). This process of creating new knowledge is the 'cognitive praxis' of social movements, and it is through this process (which includes both knowledge production and action) that a collective identity is formed and that new forms of self-knowledge and social knowledge are produced. The cognitive approach focuses on transformation and change and views organizing activities as processes in formation. 'Cognitive praxis' is constituted of 'forms of activity by which individuals create new kinds of social identities' (ibid.: 2). There is a dialectic interaction between action and knowledge transformation. Action is both the outcome and the source of identity and knowledge transformation – 'action is forged through the construction of new consciousness and identities at the collective level' and at the same time, 'new forms of consciousness and new identities, both individual and collective, are also the product and praxis of feminist political action' (Roseneil 1995: 136).

❧ Providing new information

In Chapter Three of the present volume, Chen Yiyun explains that when she started her work in the late 1980s, the ideologically and politically based information that people were receiving from party-state institutions such as the Women's Federation and the Trade Union was insufficient to cover their need for knowledge in the reform period. One of the reasons that she started her work was that she believed there was a need to provide information to people in a 'scientific manner' as opposed to this ideologically and politically based information. Chen Yiyun points to the very central question of gender inequality, which was explained within Chinese society as a class problem, and she says: 'We have to explain that there is no scientific basis for inequality. Inequality cannot be explained on the basis of women's physical weakness. But no one used to say this in

China – not even the Women's Federation.' Through hotlines, face-to-face counselling, training sessions, meetings and publications the three organizations provide information on issues such as legal rights, marriage and family matters, sexuality, reproductive health and bringing up children, and in the case of the Migrant Women's Club, also on practical skills in coping with urban life and making a living. The need for information on these issues reflects a society undergoing rapid change, also in terms of norms: people are at a loss as to which forms of behaviour are acceptable. They are also unsure of how they can, should and want to act in relation to issues such as divorce and extramarital relations, as these take on new meanings in the context of relaxed party-state control and the expansion of market economy.

Sex education, mainly for adolescents, is one of the topics the Jinglun Family Centre has been active in promoting. Since the 1950s–1960s, manuals on human reproduction have been published as part of the population control programmes, but apart from these there was generally a severe lack of basic information on sex and sexuality in Chinese society at the time that it entered into the economic reforms. In the period from 1949 to 1978 'real sex education for adolescents was practically nonexistent' (Ng and Haeberle 1997: 555). Not only was information scarce, but when materials such a popular *Common Knowledge of Physiological Hygiene for Youth* were published in the 1980s, they included decidedly false information, leading young people to believe that sex was evil and dangerous and would harm their contribution to society (Dikötter 1995: 182). In the period from 1979 to 1983 as '[s]exual misconduct in the young increased, with students participating in more dating and sexual activities', authorities decided that sex education was needed (Ng and Haeberle 1997: 555) and 'the state was promoted as an agent responsible for providing the individual with the knowledge necessary to discipline his sexual economy and regulate the flow of his bodily fluids' (Dikötter 1995: 183).[2]

A meeting held in Beijing in 1997 by the Women's Committee of the Western Returned Scholars' Association (*Oumei tongxuehui*) on the topic of breast cancer illustrated to me how desperate people

2. For an overview of the discourse on and studies of sex and sexuality in contemporary China, see an interview with Pan Suiming, professor at the Institute for Sexological Research at the People's University in Beijing in Sigley and Jeffreys (1999), especially its extensive footnote references. See also Evans 1997.

were to obtain basic information on this issue. It is not really possible to determine how representative this particular meeting and its participants were of the general levels of information and knowledge in Chinese society. Still, one might assume that an organization for scholars who have returned to China from abroad houses a highly-educated segment of the population which has been exposed to knowledge and information not readily available in China at that time. Thus, a significant lack of knowledge and opportunities to acquire information, even within such a group, would point to a dire lack of information within the population in general. The presentation made by a medical doctor at the meeting was informative, but void of any gender awareness, and sprinkled with what (to my mind) were sexist comments on breasts. Nonetheless, the all-female audience was extremely enthusiastic about the talk and eager to ask questions. Their questions revealed how little access there was to both information and professional treatment. Several women described what they thought might be symptoms of breast cancer and one woman whose mother had suffered from the disease was afraid that she had also contracted it, but apparently the hospital attached to her work unit did not have the facilities to examine her. She described to the doctor how one of her breasts was sore and swollen and asked where she could obtain more information and where she should go to be examined. Other women asked how they could make appointments for examinations at the doctor's hospital. It turned out that his hospital had a mobile cancer clinic and the meeting concluded with an agreement that he would bring the clinic to a future Association meeting.

Work on legal literacy for migrant women by the Migrant Women's Club is based on the realization that members of the Club and readers of the Magazine in general lack basic knowledge of their rights – and even of the very fact that they *have* rights. For example, activities done by *Rural Women Knowing All* on the issue of suicide among rural women developed when attention was drawn to the issue by letters from these women. Globally, male suicides predominate. An exception to this is found in rural China, where female suicide rates are, on the average, 1.3 times higher than those of males (World Health Organization 1999: v). Suicide is a response that women choose when confronted with seemingly unresolvable situations, such as violence inflicted by family members. Moreover, it is not uncommon that only suicide will effectively call the attention of the authorities and the legal system to a woman's situation and lead to the persecution of her attackers (Gilmartin 1990). A study of suicide was undertaken in collaboration with doctors at a Beijing hospital, the aims being to understand why women commit suicide, and how to prevent it. In 1999 a report was published (see Xie Lihua and Song Meiya 1999b). Liu Dongxiao (1999: 16) notes that the ACWF has prohibited the sale of the report. The provision of sex education and dissemination of medical and legal information by the three organizations must be seen within this context of extreme lack of access to the most basic information and of misinformation shrouded in politically motivated discourses.[3]

In the case of sex education, the organizations took up the issue and involved themselves in the debate at a time when the authorities had decided that education should be provided. They contributed with specific, concrete information. In the process of providing services, engaging in research and taking part in international exchange, their discourses have begun to differ from those promoted by the authorities. Perspectives have changed and have – for some activists and organizations – become based on gender awareness and women's needs.

✂ Organizing as a learning process

The Women's Hotline provides an example of how the contents and attitudes of counselling change during the process of organizing. Activists did not start out with the intent to provide counselling based on a gender perspective. However, gradually, gender awareness has, as Wang Xingjuan explains in Chapter Two, become a requirement when recruiting and training new volunteers. There are differences of opinion concerning the importance of this requirement among Hotline supervisors, and while some give counselling based on a gender perspective, others base their responses to callers on what Wang Xingjuan calls 'traditional ideology'. The fact that Wang Xingjuan and some Hotline supervisors emphasize the importance of gender awareness does not mean that this can be effectuated automatically. According to Women's Hotline supervisor Wang Fengxian 'Development of gender awareness is a process. I did not have gender awareness when I started at the Hotline. Generally, Hotline supervisors agree that gender awareness training is important, but the process takes time.' When the Women's Health Network translated *Our Bodies, Ourselves*, published by the Boston Women's Health

---

3. See Wan Yanhai (2000) on collaboration between party-state institutions and the International Education Foundation/Unification Church in advocating chastity education and opposing safe sex education as a means to avoiding HIV/AIDS.

Collective, the translators had many discussions and often disagreed severely on the usefulness of the attitudes of the book, for example on the question of homosexuality. When the Chinese version (see Liu Bohong 1998) was published, the chapters on homosexuality were censored by the authorities, and it took several years to find a publisher who dared to print the book at all. Knowledge on specific issues has been changing. More importantly, the overall under-standing among activists themselves of the role of gender in society at large is changing from one of biologically determined to one of socially constructed gender-based roles. Since the early 1990s, among the many courses and conferences on women's studies and activist training workshops for which donor organizations have helped to provide trainers, one workshop was special. It took place in 1998 over several sessions, and had the aim of writing a gender and development training manual. It also used the same participatory procedures that came to be used in future training based on the manual (Bu *et al.* 1999) and resulted in the establishment of a Gender and Development Facilitator Group, which has since then travelled to many provinces to provide gender awareness training courses.

International exchange has done a great deal to introduce gender perspectives and awareness, and to inspire new viewpoints. It is interesting that Wang Xingjuan points to a meeting in India as *the* event that led her to realize the importance of gender awareness. About a year before the meeting, a group of three British academics and activists held a training workshop for Women's Hotline counsellors based on perspectives similar to those that Wang Xingjuan says she first really 'heard' in India. This example points to organizing as a learning process – a transformative practice. Once they came into direct contact with individual women through counselling, empirical research and other activities, activists realized that the problems confronting women were often more complex than they had initially realized. Moreover, additional problems that they had not considered were brought to light, as when WRI research on prostitution revealed that a considerable number of prostitutes were adolescent girls, that they had received practically no sex education and that they were often victims of sexual abuse (Hongfeng 1998: 5). In the process of providing services and engaging in research, perceptions of what constitutes 'objective, scientific' knowledge changed, and official discourses were challenged. Terminologies have changed and 'new' views on and understanding of 'old' issues have emerged.

❧ Violence against women

Chen Yiyun says that she and her colleagues were astonished to find that domestic violence existed at all in Chinese society. The Women's Research Institute became aware of the problems of sexual harassment and domestic violence when Hotline callers asked about these issues, and new ways of understanding them were introduced via contacts to the international women's movements. A 'White Paper on Domestic Violence' written by Pi Xiaoming and published in 1991 is one of the first major statements referred to by women's movement activists as an indication that men's domestic violence against women began at that time to be publicly recognized and addressed in China. The paper was published by the Women's Federation journal, *Women in China* (*Zhongguo funü*), after having been rejected by a Beijing newspaper.[4] A couple of years later, a great deal of media debate on domestic violence was created by a case that was widely publicized by the Trade Union Department of Women Workers in cooperation with the *Workers' Daily*. It concerned a woman worker in Sichuan province whose husband cut off her nose and ears. Despite protests by the husband's work-unit, the Department took the husband to court on behalf of the wife.

Growing awareness and public recognition of the issue was also reflected in the early 1990s by surveys on women's status, marriage and family relations that included questions on domestic violence, and in other surveys specifically aimed at investigating the extent and background of domestic violence in China. Gradually, over the past ten years or so, the issue of men's violence against women has become more and more visible in the public debate. It is not possible to determine to what degree popular organizing by women has made this happen, but there is no doubt that some of it is due to activists' work in making an unrecognized problem visible and challenging conventional attitudes that have hitherto accepted domestic violence as something 'natural' and private. In 1994 Wang Xingjuan spoke of women being beaten (*ouda*) by their husbands. A few years later she was speaking of domestic violence (*jiating baoli*) – a concept introduced to China via the United Nations Women's Conferences and other international exchange. Based on a study of the Women's Research Institute Women's Hotline, Virginia Cornue suggests that the new organization activity be defined as 'a new form of statist public sphere in which women's NGOs function in a blended relationship with the state' (Cornue 1999: 86). Cornue notes that 'neither

---

4. For the story of the rejection, see Cai, Feng and Guo 2001.

radically different definitions of *nüxing* [women] nor feminisms are being discussed in China' (1999: 83) and that 'what was being maneuvered and strategized was not what "women" mean or do, or even how women's emancipation should be achieved, but who would achieve women's emancipation. What emerged then, was not so much a debate over values and goals but a competition over public recognition and trust of the institutional entity that would engineer women's emancipation' (ibid.: 83–84). Finally, Cornue concludes that for a nonstatist public women's sphere to develop, the personal must be politicized so that women 'perceive their problems as collective social problems of women rather than just as personal ones' (ibid.: 88). The change of terminology on violence against women reflects a change of perspective in which the issue is being defined not as an individual problem but as a reflection of broader unequal gender relations in society. This may not have been happening in the early years of the Hotline; however, it is what Wang Xingjuan describes as important in the late 1990s.

All three organizations have been involved in activities concerned with the issue of violence against women, and particularly domestic violence, with the aim of linking the provision of assistance to individual women with lobbying for social change both in terms of changing attitudes and practices in society in general and changing laws and policies. Their work on violence against women – one of many issues that have been addressed – illustrates how the three organizations have developed (in different directions) in terms of both their understandings of gender-based social issues and their practices.

In the years up to 1998, the three organizations had engaged in the following activities related to the issue of violence against women:

- The Women's Research Institute/Maple Women's Psychological Counselling Centre and the Jinglun Family Centre provided psychological and legal hotline and face-to-face counselling to victims of violence.
- The Jinglun Family Centre provided refuge for battered women in their offices for a short period of time.
- The Jinglun Family Centre and the Migrant Women's Club provided practical assistance to victims of gender-based violence by helping women to receive medical care and legal aid.
- The Women's Research Institute engaged in research on domestic violence.
- The Jinglun Family Centre attempted to set up a shelter for battered women to help individual women and, based on their

cases, to research the issue and create awareness among the authorities of the problem.

- The Jinglun Family Centre set up a domestic violence hotline.
- The Migrant Women's Club and magazine *Rural Women Knowing All* provided assistance to individual victims of violence and at the same time, based on their stories, knowledge of the issue was spread to all readers of the magazine.
- The Migrant Women's Club undertook a study of and published a book on suicide among rural women.

For Chen Yiyun and the Jinglun Family Centre, difficulties encountered in relation to the 1994–95 activities on domestic violence no doubt played an important role in the decision to downplay 'intervention' (*ganyu*) activities and define the work of the Centre as primarily educational. The Centre lacked the financial and activist resources necessary to engage in direct support to women, and the issue of violence was seen as too politically sensitive. To address that particular issue in the early and mid-1990s in the form of direct services could have jeopardized all Centre activities. Chen Yiyun therefore decided to focus on educational activities instead. Her rationale was that while direct 'intervention' services could only help a limited number of individuals, the Centre would be able to reach out – via the mass media and educational materials – to a much larger segment of the population. Finding a balance between direct services and preventive education had been a problem for the Centre ever since its start and was probably resolved with the establishment of an information center. In 2000 the Centre closed one of the two offices and moved the bulk of activities to the Adolescent Sexual Health Education and Information Centre.[5] The intervention activities that have been carried out since 1995 are related to much less politically sensitive issues such as sex education for adolescents. With the Information Centre, the Jinglun Family Centre has found a mode of action that suits both its decision to focus on education, and the ad-hoc nature of activist relations to the Centre.

Early Women's Research Institute engagement in the issue of violence against women was less politically sensitive than the activities of the Jinglun Family Centre. Although the Institute's plans to include a paper researching domestic violence at its NGO Forum workshop en-

---

5. The new centre, which is located at the China Children's Centre (*Zhongguo ertong zhongxin*), publishes an adolescent education newsletter, *Qing pingguo* [Green Apple]. For more information, see http://www.Greenapple.org.cn.

countered difficulties (as described in Chapter Two), the Institute was not involved in providing direct support to victims to the same degree as the Jinglun Family Centre. Apart from the early research project on domestic violence, the Institute did not seriously address the issue until the late 1990s, when Wang Xingjuan became involved in plans to set up a network of organizations working specifically on the issue of violence against women. The Migrant Women's Club is also a member of this new network, to which I shall return later in this chapter.

Cooperating with party-state institutions – a requirement and a mode of action

Popular women's organizations do not possess institutionalized power. There are no established formal political channels designed through which they can work. Instead of the forms of protest (such as demonstrations, strikes, marches, boycotts, occupations and obstruction) typically applied by social movements in many other parts of the world to focus attention on their issues, a quite different style using indirect and non-disruptive action has been adopted by the three Beijing organizations to manoeuvre within a political context in which the authorities are unaccustomed to and suspicious of organizing from below. It should be mentioned, however, that there were attempts in 1998 by the Women's Media Watch Network to arrange a street demonstration protesting violations committed against ethnic Chinese women in Indonesia.[6] Permission to hold a demonstration was not granted, and a public meeting was held at a hotel instead. This does not mean that the new forms of organizing do not use the street space to make their activities visible, as another type of street activity has been staged by both the Jinglun Family Centre and the Women's Research Institute: both organizations have set up street counselling stands on a one-day basis in a manner similar to that used by party-state institutions. From these street stands, counselling has been provided, media coverage of the activity and the organization has been ensured and an image of the new organization as contributing to the welfare of the citizens of Beijing by offering free services has been promoted. Legitimacy is sought by imitating party-state forms of action, although the contents may differ. In general, a primary mode of action applied by popular

---

6. See Pei 1999: 29–30 for an account of dissident protests against Indonesia's treatment of ethnic Chinese.

organizations has been to establish and exploit contacts to various party-state institutions.

Party-state institutions – often the All China Women's Federation, but also several other institutions – have been involved in some way or other in nearly every activity in which the organizations have engaged. For popular organizations, cooperation with party-state institutions is, first, a way of gaining legitimacy by registration or affiliation or by making claim to party-state endorsement of the organization and its activities. Because such support could not be secured an activity such as the Jinglun Family Centre shelter was not possible. Second, cooperation is a means of establishing contact to women and the population in general via extensive party-state institutional networks. Third, cooperation is a means of influencing party-state institutions.

Gaining legitimacy: registration and affiliation

China does not really understand popular organizations. We are always being asked 'Why is this organization necessary?' Moreover, there is a continuous sense of this thing of ours being, well, not quite legal, even though we have registered formally. (Women's Research Institute activist, interview 1996)

The preceding three chapters have described the varied forms of formal affiliation and registration of the three organizations and some of the difficulties that they have encountered, first in registering and then in interacting and maintaining a relationship with their supervisory units. If one looks at additional groups, an even more diverse picture of the registration situation of popular women's organizations in Beijing emerges. Registration of so-called 'social organizations' (*shehui tuanti*) is a formal, legal requirement according to the 1989 Regulations on the Registration and Management of Social Organizations (*Shehui tuanti dengji guanli tiaoli*),[7] and is designed

---

7. See White, Howell and Shang 1996: Chapter 5, for an analysis of the policy and legal framework underlying the registration system. The Regulations on the Registration and Management of Social Organizations were first promulgated in 1989. On the same day that the revised Regulations were passed in 1998 in an attempt to bring all forms of non-profit ventures under stricter control, the State Council also promulgated the Provisional Regulations on the Registration and Management of People-Organized Non-Enterprise Units (*Minban feiqiye danwei dengji guanli zanxing tiaoli*); Provisional Regulations on the Registration and Management of Institutional Units (*Shiye danwei dengji guanli zanxing tiaoli*) were also announced, but not promulgated (Human Rights in China 1998). See Human Rights in China 1998 for a detailed assessment of the principal elements of these regulations.

to monitor, regulate and control new institutions. However, for the three organizations, their choice of issues to address, activities in which to engage and modes of action have not primarily been controlled or restricted by their supervisory body or the registration requirement as such. On the contrary, to some extent the legitimacy of registration has provided the basis for relative autonomy in determining the contents of their activism. The registration history of the three organizations illustrates how registration is linked both to the overall political situation at the time of registration and to the personal contacts activists have been able to bring into play in order to find institutions willing to act as supervisory units (*guakao danwei*) in order to secure legality via registration or, alternatively, to secure legal status without registration. Moreover, once some form of registration or affiliation has been secured, the organizations have been able to go about their business in relative independence of the supervisory body. This does not mean that no restrictions are imposed but these are not necessarily decidedly structural.

The Women's Research Institute was established in 1988 during a politically relatively relaxed period, and affiliation to the China Academy of Management Science was based on the personal contacts of one of the founding members of the Academy.[8] In 1995 when the Institute attracted the attention of the Public Security Bureau and became very politically sensitive, the supervisory unit withdrew its support rather than risk being negatively affected by the relationship. Subsequently, as described in Chapter Two, only the stubbornness and inventiveness of Wang Xingjuan ensured the survival of the organization through its transformation into the Maple Women's Psychological Counselling Centre and its registration as a private enterprise.

Chen Yiyun's first attempt at setting up the Jinglun Family Centre at the Institute of Sociology at the Chinese Academy of Social Sciences – also in 1988 – did not succeed. Subsequently, due to the increased political restrictiveness in 1989 in connection with student and worker demonstrations and the leadership's use of military forces against the demonstrators, the meetings that Chen Yiyun was holding at the Democratic League were suspended, and she decided to postpone further attempts at setting up an organization. When she tried again in 1991, she contacted the China Association of Social Workers, where she was a standing committee member. The

---

8. See also Liu Dongxiao 1999: 4–5.

Association was at first sceptical, but in 1993 Chen Yiyun applied again, and the Centre was finally registered.

The situation has been somewhat different for the Migrant Women's Club. *Rural Women Knowing All* lay within the structure of *China Women's News*, thus, the Magazine was indirectly part of the All China Women's Federation. Having the Magazine start the Club in 1996 can be viewed as a strategic choice on the part of the two main initiators, Editor Xie Lihua and Professor Wu Qing, based on their experience and knowledge of the difficulties encountered by two of the first popular women's organizations in Beijing – the Women's Research Institute and the Jinglun Family Centre. By setting up the Club within the Federation, the problems encountered by the two other organizations in finding and maintaining a supervisory unit were avoided. However, the following quote from a study by Liu Dongxiao illustrates how the ACWF as supervisory body and Xie Lihua, as the director of the Migrant Women's Club, which was set up by the magazine *Rural Women Knowing All*, have held differing views as to the autonomy of the Magazine, and thereby also of the Club:

> According to the ACWF, the RWKA [*Rural Women Knowing All*] was a financially independent unit but the editorial office was subject to the administrative leadership of the Chinese Women's News (CWN). The CWN was the official newspaper of the ACWF. It put down a one-time investment of RMB 60,000 *yuan* and allowed Xie Lihua to pick one staff member among her CWN colleagues. Xie persuaded one colleague to assist her for one year and published the first issue in 1993. The ACWF and the CWN gave Xie the autonomy to run the RWKA but did not tell her how, because it was the first magazine for rural women and nobody knew exactly how. Meanwhile, they might have supposed Xie knew the routine from her work experiences. But Xie probably took the autonomy more seriously than the routine. As Xie put it: 'it was like they gave me a permit to bear a child, but the child had to be brought up by myself'. (Liu Dongxiao 1999: 6)

In fact, the Migrant Women's Club is not actually registered as a separate entity. Xie Lihua has explained this situation as follows:

> Because we are affiliated with the major national newspaper *China Women's News*, we asked to register with the Ministry of Civil Affairs. But then we were told that we should register in Beijing, and so we asked to register with the Beijing Civil Affairs Department. They in turn told us that since we were operating more or less like a readers'

club, there was no need for registration. We could carry out our activities just in the name of the registered *China Women's News*. I had this telephone conversation recorded [audience laughter], that's why up to this moment, the Migrant Women's Club has never run into trouble.[9] (Xie Lihua in Hsiung, Jaschok and Milwertz 2001: 227).

The affiliation and registration situations of other popular women's organizations in Beijing add to a picture of the fluid and varied nature of the registration aspect of organizing. Registration, as required by the Regulations, is one of several avenues for securing a legal position. Following affiliation to a law firm, the Centre for Women's Law Studies and Legal Services is in a situation somewhat similar to that of the Migrant Women's Club. As in the case of the Women's Research Institute, the firm terminated the affiliation when the situation became politically sensitive. Since 1995 the Centre has been affiliated to Peking University. In the words of lawyer and Director Guo Jianmei:

> After our Centre started its operation, we had attracted some social attention and the Procurate came to ask us what exactly we intended to do. We were very skilful in handling that inquiry: we said that the Centre was an important classroom and basis for teachers and students of Peking University's Law Department to participate in the realization of the rule of law. That was a very safe approach; we have been using it until this day. Because of that, we have successfully avoided the troubles of registration or investigation. We are still not clear whether the Centre is legal or not, but we have been more or less free for almost three years and we're still operating very well. I suspect that we'll continue to survive that way. (Guo Jianmei in ibid.).

The Women's Media Watch Network, which was set up in 1996, is affiliated with a professional women's organization, the Capital Women Journalists' Association, where Xie Lihua, one of the initiators, was a vice-president. When the Association for Promoting Rural Women in Development registered in 1994 it was registered directly with the Beijing Bureau of Civil Affairs without intermediary affiliation to a supervisory body. A few groups, such as the East Meets West Feminist Translation Group, are not affiliated with any institution, nor are they registered. This is possible because their main activity is

---

9. More recently the relationship of the magazine to the Women's Federation has become more complicated, and the magazine is attempting to detach itself from the Federation (Liu Dongxiao 1999: 10, 25).

to conduct discussions between members themselves, and because they were fortunate enough to have access to meeting places that did not involve using the facilities of party-state institutions.

Registration is important for popular organizations as a means of acquiring legality and some degree of legitimacy. The authorities utilize the Regulations as an effective way of controlling organizing and excluding unwanted forms of social organizing. Although perhaps not representative, the case of a group of laid-off women workers who attempted to register an organization in the late 1990s by affiliating it to one of the already registered popular women's organizations when no other supervisory unit or affiliation could be found, underlines the importance of exploiting established contacts to party-state institutions in order to register.[10] The women workers did not have established contacts to a party-state institution that was willing to act as supervisory body; therefore, they turned to the popular organizations, who were, however, not willing to accept them as affiliates. This was partly because their own situations were already politically insecure (thus they would risk attracting attention which might jeopardize their own activities), and partly because the organizers were workers, and not intellectuals.[11] However, registration according to the Regulations on Social Organizations is not the only way to attain legitimacy, as illustrated by organizations such as the Migrant Women's Club and the Centre for Women's Law Studies and Legal Service, neither of which is registered according to the Regulations. Their legitimacy is achieved through affiliation with party-state institutions – the All China Women's Federation's *China Women's News* and the Law Department at Peking University. These affiliations are based on the contacts of the two directors who are themselves 'members' of the host institutions. Xie Lihua is an ACWF employee. Guo Jianmei's link as a former student of the Law Department at Peking University is less clear; however, the co-founder of the Centre, Ma Yinan, teaches at the department. Based primarily on personal contacts, organizations, groups and networks have used various forms of affiliation or formal registration in order to legalize their

---

10. See Perry (2001) and Jaschok (1998). Both point to the importance of *guanxi* – contacts, connections and personal networks – in paving the way for the new forms of bottom-up organizing.

11. The women who have organized are primarily intellectuals (*zhishi fenzi*) meaning that they are educated as journalists, doctors, engineers and scientists, university lecturers and professors. They work for other women including intellectuals, workers and rural women.

activities. However, affiliation and registration is fragile, and supervisory units are only willing to provide legality as long as this does not pose any threat to their own position. Moreover, even when registration has been achieved, there is a constant pressure on the organizations (more specifically on the founders/directors) to secure and ensure continued legality. This is vividly illustrated by the case of the Women's Research Institute, which was nearly shut down in 1995 following the termination of its affiliation by the Chinese Academy of Management Science. Subsequently, the Institute registered as a private enterprise under a new name and without a supervisory unit. Since its establishment the Jinglun Family Centre has been affiliated to the China Association of Social Workers. Although the relationship seems to have been relatively unproblematic and the Association even provided financial support to the Centre when it was first set up, Chen Yiyun has continuously been under the pressure of not knowing whether the Association might suddenly terminate the agreement. Chen Yiyun was especially worried about the possibility of this happening in connection with the revision of the Regulations on Social Organizations and in connection with a critique of the donor organization from which the Centre was receiving funding. Chen Yiyun therefore felt pressured to plan and strategize to find an alternative supervisory unit should the Association terminate the relationship. Not until a new director, who was supportive of the JFC and of popular organizing in general, was appointed to the Association in 1998 did Chen Yiyun think the Centre was relatively secure.

In conclusion, the three organizations are registered or affiliated in three different ways: the Jinglun Family Centre according to the Regulations, the Maple Women's Psychological Counselling Centre as a private enterprise and the Migrant Women's Club as part of the ACWF. Registration requirements are primarily a party-state means of controlling and restricting popular organizing. Successful registration can be used to gain a certain limited legitimacy. Importantly, some form of registration or affiliation is a prerequisite for receiving donor funding and for joining some activities, such as when the Women's Research Institute held a workshop at the Women's Conference NGO Forum. Restrictions on the autonomy of popular organizing are to a high degree to be found in the intangible and invisible political context in general. Activists are extremely sensitive to the boundaries imposed on popular organizing, and one of the great burdens in bearing responsibility for an organization lies in the insecurity and shifting nature of what Liu Dongxiao (1999: 9) has appropriately termed the 'erratic political harassment' of popular forms of organizing. If restrictions were clearly defined and fixed, then it would be much less strenuous to deal with them. As it is, they practically hit activists arbitrarily out of the blue and are 'contingent upon government campaigns or other idiosyncratic events' (ibid.). The organizations are engaged in innovative forms of organizing from below and are continuously pushing and shifting the boundaries of what is tolerated by the authorities. At the same time they generally impose a large measure of self-restriction upon themselves, and they are extremely careful to cross the invisible lines of the acceptable in tiny, gradual steps.

Gaining legitimacy beyond registration and exploiting networks

Beyond registration or affiliation with party-state institutions, one way of gaining legitimacy and crossing boundaries without seeming to do so is to invite prominent leaders of party-state institutions to endorse organization events. For example, All China Women's Federation leaders have given their support to activities held by all three organizations by attending meetings and conferences where they have given speeches of support and by acting as advisors to various organization activities. The advisor role does not necessarily entail any practical work but mainly plays a symbolic role. As Liu Dongxiao has pointed out, these symbols of party-state support are mainly produced for party-state institutions in the sense that '[a]n official of junior level will think to himself/herself: since my leader is supporting the cause, why should I be suspicious?' (ibid.: 12). In 1995 when the Jinglun Family Centre started a hotline on domestic violence, the activity was legitimized by using the coming Women's Conference logo in the announcement in the *Workers' Daily*.

Of the three organizations, the Migrant Women's Club, by nature of its establishment within the framework of the All China Women's Federation, has had the easiest access to cooperation with a party-state institution. The Club is able to use its status as an ACWF activity to gain access to rural women by cooperating with village and county level Federation cadres. Just as the All China Women's Federation uses its status as an NGO in international contexts and its status as a party-state organization in the domestic context (Naihua Zhang 2001), the Club perceives of itself as an NGO or popular organization, but uses its ACWF status when this is opportune. In comparison with the WRI/MWPCC, the Jinglun Family Centre has been in a privileged position to create and nurture working relations with party-state institutions. Wang Xingjuan had retired when the Women's Research Institue was established, but when Chen Yiyun established the JFC, she was employed as a sociologist by a party-state institution – the Chinese Academy of Social Sciences (CASS) – and she continued in this position for the following eight years, until 2000. Chen Yiyun mentions that her status as an academic played an important role in creating her image as a well-known family and marriage counsellor among the public. It was also her status as an academic employed by a party-state institution which provided access to collaboration with party-state institutions. Chen Yiyun's evaluation of her own position in relation to Wang Xingjuan's is as follows:

> Wang Xingjuan's organization is a purely popular organization, which is more or less similar to the JFC, but her centre is at the same time not quite similar. She does not have the party-state networks that we have to help her. I have often recommended Wang Xingjuan to the Women's Federation but they will not accept her, perhaps because of something that happened in connection with the Women's Conference. Hillary Clinton wanted to visit the Women's Research Institute Hotline and there was also some trouble once with the Security Bureau. So the networks that I work with are afraid to cooperate with Wang Xingjuan. They are afraid that there will be trouble again. Another reason is that Wang Xingjuan has retired. Because I work at the Chinese Academy of Social Sciences, people feel more secure because I have a boss to control me. Wang Xingjuan is not under any control. (Chen Yiyun, interview 1998)

Wang Xingjuan's view of the access of her organization to party-state institutions falls in line with Chen Yiyun's when she explains:

> We are also very willing to work with the government, but they don't necessarily want to cooperate with us. This is partly due to the circumstances of individuals. Chen Yiyun is a member of the Trade Union Women Workers Department, so they trust her. If I contact them they will feel that they already have many specialists so they would not necessarily be supportive. I have contacted Tang Kebi, but she was not really interested, so then I withdrew. Chen Yiyun has lots of contact with them, they feel that that contact is useful to them and they have good cooperation. So this is also one possibility. Some organizations can receive even more government support. I feel this is good. My organization cannot achieve this form of government support but this is still what we are striving to achieve. My aim is that society will gradually understand us and our activities. In the end the government will inevitably change its attitude. (Wang Xingjuan, interview 1998)

Chen Yiyun is, as mentioned, a member of the council of the China Association of Social Workers. She is also a council member of the Trade Union Women Workers' Department, and she has used these links not only to register the Jinglun Family Centre, but also to carry out Centre activities. The JFC has worked with institutions such as the Trade Union, provincial and lower administrative levels of the Women's Federation, the State Family Planning Commission, the State Education Commission, and the Association of Social Workers. Initially, the JFC made contact to provincial levels of the Women's Federation and the Trade Union by sending out a circular announcing the establishment of the Centre. Since then many collaborative projects have been undertaken, and in 1998 the Centre was in a position where it no longer needed to advertise but was being contacted by a number of party-state institutions wishing to initiate collaboration.

For Chen Yiyun the aim has been to work with party-state institutions to implement activities by using their networks, for as she says, '[o]ur resources are intellectual and their resources are a network. We should cooperate rather than compete'. Wang Xingjuan voices a similar opinion when she explains why she submitted a membership application on behalf of the WRI to the ACWF in September 1988. Subsequently, ACWF secretary general Guan Tao interviewed representatives of the WRI and approved the application (Women's Research Institute 1995: 3). The reason that the WRI became a group member was, according to Wang Xingjuan:

> Because we were all 'doing women', all researching women, I thought that the more closely we united, the better. Otherwise our strength would be too weak. The All China Women's Federation has a very extensive contingent of 80–100 thousand cadres. Stretching from the Central Committee to the lowest levels of administration, and from the cities to rural areas, they have cadres at all levels. They have a system. This system is very useful. We do not have this. We are just a few people – about 100 volunteer counsellors. The work we can do is extremely limited. But if we linked up our strength with their strength then we could do something. (Wang Xingjuan, interview 1996)

In terms of their relationship with the All China Women's Federation, the three organizations differ. The Migrant Women's Club, as an ACWF organization, has had the easiest access to cooperation, but has also, as Liu Dongxiao (1999: 10) has noted, been controlled more than other popular organizations. The Jinglun Family Centre has had many links to several other party-state organizations and has mainly worked with lower levels of the Federation. Of the three, the

WRI/MWPCC seems to have had the most complicated relationship with the ACWF. When the WRI held its inaugural meeting, the ACWF secretary general attended the meeting and 'expressed the hope that the appearance of more and more non-governmental women's organizations would initiate the research and development of women's studies. Guan Tao expressed her hopes that the WRI would not only become an active theoretical resource, but also a source of knowledge and information for ACWF' (Women's Research Institute 1995). High-level ACWF cadres have continuously supported WRI and MWPCC activities, but there have also been less amiable inter-actions, such as when the WRI in 1995 lost its position as a group member of the ACWF.

Influencing party-state institutions.

The aim of cooperating with party-state institutions has also been to influence these in the process of working with them. The focus has been on 1) changing their internal educational and other practices, 2) influencing party-state institutions to influence policymakers and 3) influencing party-state institutions to accept popular forms of organizing. Chen Yiyun says:

> In all our educational activities we work with party-state institutions. We bring our ideas into the process of our cooperation and we influence them from below. Officials do not have any ideology concerning marriage and family. They need an ideology. The ideology they have is political and empty. (Chen Yiyun, interview 1998)

When Chen Yiyun invited the director of the Beijing Family Planning Commission and the president of the Education Department of the State Family Planning Commission to join a delegation to Sweden to learn about sex education and visit youth centres sponsored by the Swedish International Development Cooperation Agency (Sida) the aim was twofold. According to Chen Yiyun, it was to allow representatives of party-state institutions to 'see how NGOs can function and how sex education should be introduced into family planning education.' Apparently, the aims were fulfilled, for upon returning to China, the State Family Planning Commission invited three JFC experts to give talks to staff members at their headquarters, and the JFC was invited to join a group of experts going to Zhejiang province. Chen Yiyun explains that 'the NGO role' played by the Jinglun Family Centre in relation to the State Education Commission is based on several factors. First, the JFC can provide expert knowledge that is not available within the party-state institution. Second, experts based in an outside institution are more free and can be more daring and critical than employees of the institution itself, who risk reprimands if they point at weaknesses within the system. Third, the popular organization can exploit what Chen Yiyun defines as an unhealthy cultural habit of believing that outsiders possess knowledge that is superior to inside knowledge.

Even though they have had success in influencing party-state organizations, Chen Yiyun does not think that a popular organization can influence the central government. What can be done is to influence local levels of government indirectly, so that change will gradually take place, from the district government level to that of the city, the province and so on. The Jinglun Family Centre has increasingly focused on working with party-state institutions to use their channels for creating change. By publishing with the State Education Commission the JFC can, according to Chen Yiyun, 'spread our ideas through their textbooks. They print hundreds of millions of copies, so there would be a great impact'. Influence can also be generated from below, as when the JFC pointed out the special circumstances of laid-off single mothers to the Trade Union and suggested that work be done to implement policies in support of them. Chen Yiyun points out that although the JFC does not have any channels through which to influence the People's Congress and central government directly, new channels are continuously being found, as when she became deputy director of the Department of Women at the Democratic League – a position which provided the opportunity to put forward law proposals directly to the People's Political Consultative Conference and the People's Congress. Both Xie Lihua and Wang Xingjuan are more sceptical when it comes to measuring the influence that their organizations have had. They do, however, not doubt that they have made some impact in changing attitudes and creating awareness of problems in society. Wang Xingjuan stresses that many activities have been undertaken and that the consequence in the long run must be that 'the government cannot ignore our existence. Society has to acknowledge the value of our existence'.

Collectivity and Commitment

Cooperation with one particular party-state institution – the media – has been particularly important to the development of popular women's organizing. Although 'movement events' are non-disruptive, activists are dependent on the media to transmit their activities to the general public and the authorities, as they are in other parts of the world. Both Wang Xingjuan and Chen Yiyun point to the role of the media in promoting their activities. When the WRI established its first Women's Hotline, many volunteer counsellors were journalists who gave extensive publicity to the Women's Hotline in their newspapers, magazines and other media. When the Jinglun Family Centre set up a domestic violence hotline, this was in collaboration with three other institutions, among which was the *Workers' Daily*. All three organizations have cooperated with *China Women's News* – the ACWF newspaper. For example: during the second year of the Women's Hotline *China Women's News* published a regular column with examples of Hotline calls and the advice given, and every issue printed the Hotline phone number. When the Women's Research Institute held the First National Symposium on Women's Political Participation, *China Women's News* ran a special column on women's participation in politics.[12] The Migrant Women's Club is in itself an example of the close relationship between popular organizing and the media, and Xie Lihua has been at the centre of much of the cooperation between *China Women's News* and the two other popular organizations. Cooperation with the media illustrates a blurred and fluid border dividing cooperation between popular organizations and party-state institutions on the one hand, and cooperation between popular organizations and activists in popular organizing who are situated as employees within a party-state institution on the other. Although there are no statistics available on the number of activists engaged in popular organizing and their employment situations, most are quite probably party-state employees, and many are media workers.[13] Activists working within the party-state media exploit this position in order to promote the social movement agenda. As a result, the social movement does not follow a clear delineation between popular organization and party-state organization. This manner of using the media from within is one way of applying the main social movement resources – activist commitment and active

---

12. The column 'My view on participation in politics' (*Wo de canzhengguan*) was printed from December 1991 to June 1992.
13. Results of an ongoing study on women's popular organizing in Beijing by Bu Wei and Cecilia Milwertz will provide information on the employment of activists in popular women's organizing in Beijing.

participation – in the indirect and non-disruptive mode of action adopted by popular women's organizing.[14]

Another feature of activists' commitment and active participation is that the main organizers and initiators of the three organizations, as well as other activists, are connected in a community of cooperation and exchange. The following are examples of some of the people-connections which link the three organizations and other types of activities together in a social movement.

When the Women's Research Institute was established in 1988, Xie Lihua was among the initiators and she acted as one of the first deputy directors. When the Institute established the Singles' Weekend Club, both Chen Yiyun and Xie Lihua were advisors, and when the Institute set up its first Women's Hotline, one of the experts invited to give talks on marriage and family issues to the volunteer counsellors was Chen Yiyun. Chen Yiyun's entrance to popularity was facilitated by her attendance at a meeting held by Xie Lihua at *China Women's News*. There she met radio journalist Wang Yongchen, who produced a series of radio talks with her. Later, Wang Yongchen became deputy director of the Centre. Xie Lihua was also a member of the first Jinglun Family Centre council and she set up classes for girls together with Chen Yiyun (Xie Lihua 1995d). Many other activists are involved in this intricate network of relations, which, to reiterate Dahlerup's definition, forms part of the social movement 'entity of activities by organizations, groups and followers who share a commitment to a common cause'. For example, Professor Wu Qing, who initiated the Migrant Women's Club with Xie Lihua, was one of the initiators of one of the first discussion groups on gender issues in Beijing, the Women's Studies Forum at the Beijing Foreign Studies University, where she taught English until her retirement. When the Migrant Women's Club was set up, Wu Qing was also advisor to several popular women's organizing activities, including Pi Xiaoming's Legal Advice Service and the Women's Research Institute Women's Hotline and Singles' Weekend Club. Besides, she was president of the China Women's Health Network. The web of relationships extends beyond the three organizations to other popular organizations, groups and networks, and importantly, into the All China Women's Federation.

---

14. It is, however, not always clear when popular activists exploit the media or when the media and authorities appropriate stories of popular organizing to promote an image of freedom and a multitude of popular organizing in the English-language, Chinese-published media. See, for example, Chen Ya 1995.

When the Women's Research Institute was established, the initiator group included several ACWF employees. Xie Lihua is, as has already been mentioned, employed by the ACWF newspaper *China Women's News*. Another initiator of the Women's Research Institute, who was among the five main contributors of the initial WRI funding, was also an ACWF employee. These activists did not represent the ACWF, but were engaged in popular organizing on an individual basis. A few other examples of ACWF employees who have been actively involved in popular organizing include the lawyer Pi Xiaoming from a Beijing district Women's Federation, who started the Legal Advice Service with the Women's Health Network, and Vice-President Luo Xiaolu of the Beijing Women's Federation, who started the Association for Promoting Rural Women in Development. Many others could be mentioned.

Although their views may not reflect the entire group of volunteers, interviews with nine volunteer Women's Hotline counsellors, all but one employed by party-state institutions, show that motives for working for a popular organization seem to vary along a continuum. At one end there are counsellors who wish to offer support to vulnerable women who have nowhere else to seek help. They seem neither to consider that there might be implications in working for a popular organization, nor that there is any particular reason to work with such an organization. Moving along the continuum, there is a wish to provide support and also to move away from dependency on the party-state. One volunteer states: 'In the past, individuals in China depended on the government to arrange everything for them. Now we are beginning to depend on ourselves. This is a turning point.' Finally, at the other end of the continuum are volunteers who even more explicitly espouse a political perspective in their activist engagement. One activist, who has been engaged in WRI/MWPCC work since the first Hotline opened in 1992 expresses it thus:

> I joined because I wanted to take part in the combination of counsel-ling and research. My activism is part of a vision of a Chinese society in which people are not just working ants. There should be respect for human rights and freedom of the media. I originally had enormous expectations of the WRI as a non-official organization. When I receive calls from women who have been sexually harassed at work, I feel powerless. I want to tell the women to leave their jobs. But then, what would they live on? I sometimes find it very difficult to counsel – I mean, how can there be respect for women's rights in a society that does not respect human rights in general? (Beijing activist, March 1997)

On the one hand, activists emphasize that '[p]eople feel that there is no need for NGOs. "The government can take care of everything. Why would we want NGOs?"' (WRI activist 1996), and as Chen Yiyun describes in Chapter Three, when she was trying to set up the Jinglun Family Centre, people would wonder why she was getting mixed up in matters which to their minds were, strictly speaking, within the purview of the party-state. On the other hand, and in contrast to such perceptions, activists (including those who are ACWF employees) emphasize how popular organizing on their own initiative gives them enormous possibilities to independently realize their commitment to creating social change by defining activities and identifying issues they believe should be addressed.

From its start, the Women's Research Institute Women's Hotline has included ACWF employees among its volunteers – one was head of the ACWF International Liaison Department. One of the first JFC activities was hotline and face-to-face psychological counselling managed by teachers at the Social Work Department of the Administration College for Women Cadres,[15] which is an ACWF-led institution. Several of those teachers not only later became WRI Women's Hotline counsellors, they also set up other popular organizing activities, including support groups for single mothers, based at the College under the auspices of the Women's Counselling and Development Centre. There are several examples of how these links of collaboration between activists and organizations have led to the formation of new groups, organizations and networks. When the Women's Media Watch Network was set up in 1996, Xie Lihua was involved as one of the initiators together with, among others, journalist Feng Yuan, who also took part in the meetings prior to the establishment of the WRI. One of the newest groups is a small reading and discussion group, the Gender Study Group set up by members of the Media Watch Network and the East Meets West Group, as well as the aforementioned Gender and Development Facilitator Group.

Consolidation

One of the focal points for discussions among activists from different groups has been the East Meets West Feminist Translation Group. The group was, as described in Chapter One, originally set up to translate English-language feminist texts to Chinese, but developed

---

15. Since 1995, renamed the China Women's College.

gradually into a group where activists meet to exchange information and engage in discussion (Ge and Jolly 2001). Since 1999 the Group has only met intermittently. This has been interpreted as the result of two main coordinators having left Beijing. Alternatively, it might be interpreted as a consequence of the Group having outplayed its role as focal point for a process of consciousness raising among participants, who have since then turned their attention to activities in other, newer groups.

One of the practices of the EMW Group was to invite speakers from women's studies and popular women's organizations to talk about their work and to invite activists and scholars who returned from conferences and other visits abroad to share their experiences. At one such meeting in the summer of 1998, Guo Jianmei, director of the Centre for Women's Law Studies and Legal Services (CWLSLS), had been invited to talk about the work of the Centre. At that time, initial plans to set up a Network which would focus its activities on working against violence against women were underway, and at the meeting Guo Jianmei invited activists from the East Meets West Group and other groups to gather at the CWLSLS to discuss plans for the Network. The meeting took place in August 1998 with representatives from the Centre for Women's Law Studies and Legal Services, the East Meets West Group, the Maple Women's Psychological Counselling Centre, the Migrant Women's Club, the Media Watch Network, and other groups and individuals, including one or two from other parts of China, attending. Planning and preparations continued following the meeting, and in 2000 the Network 'Domestic Violence in China – Research, Intervention and Prevention' (hereafter the Network or Domestic Violence Network) was formally established. I would argue that the Network reflects a consolidation within the new wave of the Chinese women's movement. The links between organizations and groups from both Beijing and other parts of China which form the Network are indicative of a collectivity of activism and commitment and are a measure of movement wave success in terms of what Suzanne Staggenborg (1995: 347), in a redefining of the criteria of movement success, has defined as 'fluid outcomes'.

Not all activities in the new movement wave in Beijing have survived. Some groups and organizations have only existed for short periods of time, some did not manage to register and their activities stopped, some were closed following intervention by authorities, some due to lack of funds, some due to collaboration difficulties between initiators or differing views on aims and approaches. Activities such as the Jinglun Family Centre's attempt at setting up a shelter for battered women did not succeed, and in Shanghai a shelter for battered women was closed by authorities. Nevertheless, all these activities together have paved the way for later consolidation. In the process of developing a new wave of the Chinese women's movement, the Jinglun Family Centre has played the role of catalyst to other activities and organizations and has been an innovator in addressing issues such as domestic violence and sex education. Innovation has extended also to internal working practices. Having learnt from the experiences of activists' dissatisfaction with hierarchical working practices in some of the first organizations, the Domestic Violence Network has been at great pains to set up and maintain a democratic participatory internal working practice.

Referring to the work of Gusfield (1981) and Mueller (1987), Suzanne Staggenborg argues that feminist organizations can be considered effective if a broad definition of movement 'success' is adapted. This definition of success is based on a 'long-range processual view of social movements' in which success is measured not only in terms of policy outcomes but also in terms of the 'cultural consequences beyond the impact of their organized and public activities' (Staggenborg 1995: 341). Movements need first to challenge existing ideas, cultural practices and means of socialization, before achieving more substantial goals, and these outcomes should be treated as success. Movements can be successful in introducing new ideas and creating new norms – externally in society and internally within the movement – and these outcomes may produce subsequent achievements. Staggenborg emphasizes that this sort of 'cultural success' can typically be attributed not to any one organization, but rather to the entire movement as such. Moreover, some apparent 'failures' actually become 'successes' of a sort by contributing to later collective action because:

> Feminist organizations can be effective at the same time as they self-destruct as organizations and fail to achieve changes in public policy. Groups that are unsuccessful in terms or organizational maintainance and policy outcomes may be effective as the centres of movement communities and as the originators of cultural changes. Although the successes of many feminist organizations tend to be hidden, they are likely to have an impact on subsequent rounds of collective action. (Staggenborg 1995: 353).

Moreover, success includes 'pools of activists who remain involved in movement activities, models of collective action that are employed by subsequent activists and ideologies that continue to attract adherents' (ibid.).

Conclusion

In conclusion, we shall return to Dahlerup's definition of social movement waves in which 'mobilization is running high, many new organizations are being created, and a comprehensive debate on women's position reaches the public agenda. If successful, the movement contributes to changing the norms and values in society' (Dahlerup 2000: 27). Clearly, a process of establishing many new feminist organizations and groups started in the 1980s, and is continuing and consolidating itself ten to fifteen years later. Debates have been initiated within the movement and publicly. Internally within the wave, activists are in the process of transforming and transgressing dominant gender discourses, and they are becoming a collective with a shared identity and consciousness. The Domestic Violence Network is one reflection of a consolidation of this process. The development of the Jinglun Family Centre in a direction away from the other organizations is also part of the process of organizing. By the end of the 1990s, the Centre was no longer being defined by some Beijing activists as part of feminist organizing, primarily due to its views on issues such as homosexuality and adolescent sex education, which differ from those of activists at the cutting-edge of the wave. How activists will encompass the diversity of the wave remains to be seen. A characteristic of waves is – to borrow from DeLombard (1995: 21) – that they curve alternately in opposite directions and embody contradiction.

This study has viewed the development of organizing from the perspective of the participants. This means that no attempt has been made to determine the actual degree to which debates have been initiated publicly or to which the general public has become receptive to movement ideas, nor to gauge the extent to which the ideas of the movement are making an impact in terms of new laws. However, while activists lament the limits on their access to influencing society and the authorities, there is no doubt that incredible ingenuity has been brought into play in order to draw attention to movement issues and spread these to society at large via the media and the use of organizational publications, as well as through the many books and articles written by activists (both those who are media workers and others) on their own initiative.[16]

The situation has changed dramatically since the book *Waiguo nüquan yundong wenxuan* [*Selections from the foreign feminist movement*]

(Duan 1987), including extracts from Simone de Beauvoir's *The Second Sex*, was published as an internal publication, inaccessible to the general public. The situation has become one in which women's organizations, women's studies, and commercial publishers are selling many – both Chinese and translated – 'women' and 'gender' titles, many of which challenge dominant discourse and provide innovative emancipatory alternatives.[17] In 1999 the Gender Awareness Resource Group was set up in Beijing specifically in order to translate feminist texts into Chinese.

The three organizations studied are distinct in their organizational affiliations, their internal organizational structures and their choices of modes of action, including their types and degrees of collaborative relations with party-state institutions. Although there is variation in the values and beliefs underlying each of these three organizations, it is their commonalities in ideology and their practices of providing service, engaging in research and advocacy with the objective of improving women's lives, challenging inequality and working to create social change in gender relations that joins them as social movement actors. Together they are part of a new wave of the Chinese women's movement. They are joined in a web of relationships between activists and organizations and by their combined contributions to developing innovative interpretations and practices in the movement in a process which has entailed failures that provide part of the ground for future success. As part of an ongoing process of innovation they are strong, although they are small in numbers.

Wang Xingjuan says that 'the strength of popular women's organizing is like a drop of water – extremely tiny'.

Those drops have become part of a wave.

Movement waves have life cycles of rise, peak and decline (Dahlerup 2000) and the current wave of the Chinese women's movement is in a process of rising.

---

16. See for example three books written by Women's Hotline counsellors: Yi, Jin and Chun 1995, Wang Fengxian 1996 and Ding Ning 2000.
17. See for example Li Yinhe, Lin Chun and Tan Shen (eds) (1997) – a translation of texts by Valerie Bryson, Juliet Mitchell, Heidi Hartmann, Iris Young, Carol Gilligan, Nancy Fraser, Linda Nicholson, Joan W. Scott, Evelyn Fox Keller and Chandra Mohanty.

Appendix

POPULAR WOMEN'S ORGANIZING IN BEIJING

This list includes organizations, groups, networks and activities mentioned in this book and is therefore not a comprehensive list of popular women's organizing in Beijing.

The Ark Family Centre (1998)
方舟家庭中心
Fangzhou jiating zhongxin
Established by the Maple Women's Psychological Counselling Centre

The Association for Promoting Rural Women in Development (1993)
农村妇女发展促进会
Nongcun funü fazhan cujinhui

The Beijing Sisters (1998)
北京姐妹小组
Beijing jiemei xiaozu
Previously the Queer Women Group, *Nü tongzhi xiaozu,* 女同帧组

The Blue-stocking Group (1994)
蓝袜子小组
Lanwazi xiaozu

The Centre for Women's Law Studies and Legal Services, the Law Department, Peking University (1995)
北京大学法律学系妇女法律研究与服务中心
Beijing daxue falüxuexi funü falü yanjiu yu fuwu zhongxin

149

The China–Canada Young Women's Project (1993)
中加女青年项目
Zhongjia nü qingnian xiangmu

The East Meets West Feminist Translation Group (1993)
东西方相遇小组
Dongxifang xiangyu xiaozu

The Gender Awareness Resource Group (1999)
社会性别意识资源小组
Shehui xingbie yishi ziyuan xiaozu

The Gender and Development Facilitator Group (1999)
社会性别与发展协作者小组
Shehui xingbie yu fazhan xiezuozhe xiaozu

The (Gender) Study Group (2000)
读书小组
Dushu xiaozu

The Girls' Club (1994)
少女之家
Shaonü zhi jia
Established by the Jinglun Family Centre and the Department of Social Work at the Youth School, Qingnian zhengzhi xueyuan 青年政治学院

The Jinglun Family Centre, the China Association of Social Workers (1993)
中国社会工作协会京伦家庭科学中心
Zhongguo shehui gongzuo xiehui Jinglun jiating kexue zhongxin

The Legal Advice Service Centre (1993)
中国心理卫生协会妇女健康与发展专业委员会妇女法律服务中心
Zhongguo xinli weisheng xiehui funü jiankang yu fazhan zhuanye weiyuanhui funü falü fuwu zhongxin
Established by the Women's Health Network

The Maple Women's Psychological Counselling Centre (1996)
北京红枫妇女心理咨询服务中心
Beijing hongfeng funü xinli zixun fuwu zhongxin
Previously the Women's Research Institute (1988).

The Migrant Women's Club (1996)
打工妹之家
Dagongmei zhi jia
Established by *Rural Women Knowing All* magazine

The Network 'Domestic Violence in China – Research, Intervention
and Prevention' (2000)
反对针对妇女的家庭暴力对策研究与干预项目
Fandui zhendui funü de jiating baoli duice yanjiu yu ganyu xiangmu

The Practical Skills Training Centre for Rural Women (1999)
农家女实用技能培训学校
Nongjianü shiyong jineng peixun xuexiao
Established by Rural Women Knowing All magazine

The Singles' Weekend Club (1991)
单身周末俱乐部
Danshen zhoumo julebu
Established by the Women's Research Institute

The Tongzhi Pager Hotline / Queer Pager Hotline (1997)
同志热线
Tongzhi rexian

The Women's Counselling Activity House (1994)
妇女咨询与活动中心
Funü zixun yu huodong zhongxin
Established by the Jinglun Family Centre and the China Administration
College for Women Cadres, Zhongguo funü ganbu guanli xueyuan 中
国妇女干部管理学院

The Women's Counselling and Development Centre, the Social Work
Department at the China Women's College (originally the Women's
Counselling Activity House)
中华女子学院社会公司系女性咨询发展中心
Zhonghua nüzi xueyuan shehui gongzuoxi nüxing zixun fazhan zhongxin

The Women's Health Network, the China Mental Health Association (1993)
中国心理卫生协会妇女健康与发展专业委员会
Zhongguo xinli weisheng xiehui funü jiankang yu fazhan zhuanye weiyuanhui

The Women's Hotline (1992)
妇女热线
Funü rexian
Established by the Women's Research Institute

The Women's Media Watch Network (1996)
妇女传媒监测网络
Funü chuanmei jiance wangluo

The Women's Research Institute, the China Academy of Management Science (1988)
中国管理科学研究院妇女研究所
Zhongguo guanli kexue yanjiuyuan funü yanjiusuo

The Women's Studies Forum, Beijing Foreign Languages Institute (1985)
北京外语学院妇女沙龙
Beijing waiyu xueyuan funü shalong

Bibliography

Bao, Xiaolan with Wu Xu (2001) 'Feminist Collaboration between Diaspora and China', in Hsiung, Ping-Chun, Maria Jaschok and Cecilia Milwertz with Red Chan (eds), *Chinese Women Organizing – Cadres, Feminists, Muslims, Queers.* Oxford: Berg, 79–100.

Basu, Amrita (1995) 'Introduction', in Amrita Basu (ed.), *The Challenge of Local Feminisms: Women's Movements in Global Perspective.* Boulder, San Francisco, Oxford: Westview Press, 1–21.

Bergman, Solveig (1995) 'structural Conditions for Women's Movements. A Comparison of Finland and the Federal Republic of Germany', in Ghaiss Jasser, Meike Verloo and Margit van der Steen (eds), *Travelling through European Femisims.Cultural and Political Practices.* Utrecht. 10–26.

—— (1999) 'Kvinnor i nya sociala rörelser' [Women in new social movements], in Christina Bergqvist et al (eds), Likestilte demokratier? *Kjönn og politikk i Norden* [Equal Democracies – gender and politics in the Nordic countries]. Oslo: Universitetsforlaget, 91–110.

—— (2000) 'studying Women's Movements in a Cross-national Perspective: Dilemmas and Potentilities', in Aino Saarinen, Hilda Rømer Christensen and Beatrice Halsaa (eds), *Women's Movements and Internationalisation: the 'Third Wave'?* Oulu: Oulu University, 148–159.

Bode Ulrike (1995) 'A Conversation with Wu Qing', in Alida Brill (ed.), *A Rising Public Voice – Women in Politics Worldwide.* New York: The Feminist Press, 41–57.

Bonnin, Michel and Yves Chevrier (1991) 'Autonomy during the Post-Mao Era'. *The China Quarterly.* No 127, September, 569–593.

Brittain, Victoria and Linda Jakobsen (1995) 'China Hears the Agonised Cries of its Battered Women'. *The Guardian,* 8 September, 10.

Bu Wei, Wang Zuofang, Feng Yuan, Zhang Lixi, Du Jie and Li Huiying (1999) *Shehui xingbie yu fazhan peixun shouce* [Gender and development training manual]. Beijing: Lianheguo kaifashu zhu Hua daibiaochu.

Burton, Sandra (1990). 'Condolences, It's a Girl: China's One-Child-Per-Couple Policy Has Inflamed the Ancient Preference for Sons'. *Time.* Vol. 136, No. 19 (Fall), 36.

Bystydzienski, Jill M. and Joti Sekhon (eds), (1999) *Democratization and Women's Grassroots Movements*. Bloomington and Indianapolis: Indiana University Press.

Cai Yiping, Feng Yuan and Guo Yanqiu (2001) 'The Women's Media Watch Network', in Ping-Chun Hsiung, Maria Jaschok and Cecilia Milwertz with Red Chan (eds), *Chinese Women Organizing – Cadres, Feminists, Muslims, Queers*. Oxford: Berg.

Camauër, Leonor (2000) *Feminism, Citizenship and the Media*. Stockholm: Department of Journalism, Media and Communication, Stockholm University.

Chafetz, Janet Saltzman and Dworkin, Gary Anthony (1986) *Female Revolt. Women's Movements in World and Historical Perspective*. New Jersey: Rowman & Allenheld.

Chamberlain, Heath B. (1993) 'On the Search for Civil Society in China'. *Modern China*, Vol. 19, No. 2, April, 199–215.

—— (1994) 'Coming to Terms with Civil Society'. *The Australian Journal of Chinese Affairs*, No. 31, January, 113–117.

Charles, Nickie (1996) 'Feminist Practices. Identity, difference, power', in Nickie Charles and Felicia Huges-Freeland (eds), *Practising Feminism. Identity, Difference, Power*. London and New York: Routledge, 1–37.

Chatty, Dawn and Annika Rabo (eds), (1997) *Organizing Women – Formal and Informal Women's Groups in the Middle East*, Oxford and New York: Berg.

Chen Jingqiu (ed.), (1997) *Shaonan shaonu 100 wen* [100 teenage questions]. Beijing: Shehui kexue wenxian chubanshe.

—— (ed.), (2000) *Shaonan shaonu 100 wen* [100 teenage questions]. Beijing: Shehui kexue wenxian chubanshe.

Chen, Min (1999) 'Abused Women and Their Protection in China'. Unpublished thesis, the University of British Columbia.

Chen Ya (1995) 'Chinese NGOs in Action', in China Features (ed.), *More or Less, Half the Sky – Chinese Women Parade*. Beijing: Xinhua Publishing House, 16–19.

Chen Yiyun (1994a) *Hunyin lücheng tan you* [Exploring the secrets of marriage]. Beijing: Hongqi chubanshe.

—— (1994b) *Hunqian manbu* [A stroll before marriage]. Beijing: Hongqi chubanshe.

—— (1994c) 'Out of the Traditional Halls of Academe: Exploring New Avenues for Research on Women', in Christina K. Gilmartin, Gail Hershatter, Lisa Rofel and Tyrene White (eds), *Engendering China*. Cambridge, Massachusetts: Harvard University Press. 69–79.

—— (1994d) *Weile xia yi dai* [For the next generation]. Beijing: Hongqi chubanshe.

—— (1995) 'From Academia to Public Forum – A Woman Scholar's Road to Social Engagement', in Wong Yuenling (ed.), *Reflections and Resonance: Studies of Chinese Women Involved in International Preparatory Activities for the 1995 NGO Forum on Women*. Beijing: Ford Foundation, 32–47.

—— (2000a) *Hunyin lücheng tan you* [Exploring the secrets of marriage]. Beijing: Shehui kexue wenxian chubanshe.

—— (2000b) *Liang xing shijie hechu qu?* [Where is the world of two sexes going?]. Beijing: Shehui kexue wenxian chubanshe.

—— (2000c) *Tianya hechu mi jia'ou?* [Where to seek a perfect spouse]. Beijing: Shehui kexue wenxian chubanshe.

—— (ed.), (1994a) *Rang xingkexue zoujin jiating* [Let the science of sex enter marriage]. Beijing: Hongqi chubanshe

—— (ed.), (1994b) *Weile xia yi dai* [For the next generation]. Beijing: Hongqi chubanshe.

—— (ed.), (1997) *Xiandai hunyin yu xingkexue* [Contemporary marriage and the science of sex]. Beijing: Shehui kexue wenxian chubanshe.

Chen Yiyun, Jing Zhong, Chen Jingqiu and Huang Xiaowei (eds), (2000) *Jiedu xing de aomi* [Understanding the mystery of sex]. Beijing: Shehui kexue wenxian chubanshe.

Chen Yiyun and Lu Shizhen (eds), (1996) *Jiating yu xia yidai* [Family and the next generation]. Beijing: Shehui kexue wenxian chubanshe.

Chen Yiyun and Wang Xiufang (eds), (1997) *Qingchunqi rensheng jiaoyu shouce* [Life Education Handbook for Adolescents]. Beijing: Shehui kexue wenxian chubanshe.

—— (eds), (2000) *Dudong haizi qingchunqi* [Understanding adolescence]. Beijing: Shehui kexue wenxian chubanshe.

Christensen-Ruffman, Linda (1995) 'Women's Conceptions of the Political: Three Canadian Women's Organizations', in Myra Marx Feree and Patricia Yancey Martin (eds), *Feminist Organizations*. Philadelphia: Temple University Press, 372–393.

Cornue, Virginia (1999) 'Practising NGOness and Relating Women's Space Publicly: The Women's Hotline and the State', in Mayfair Mei-hui Yang (ed.), *Spaces of Their Own – Women's Public Sphere in Transnational China*. Minneapolis/London: University of Minnesota Press, 68–91.

Crook, Isabel, Liu Dongxiao and Lisa Stearns (1995) 'A Conversation with Wu Qing', in Alida Brill (ed.), *A Rising Public Voice – Women in Politics Worldwide*. New York: The Feminist Press at the City University of New York, 41–56.

Croll, Elisabeth (1983) *Chinese Women since Mao*. London: Zed Books.

—— (1995) *Changing Identities of Chinese Women*. Hong Kong: Hong Kong University Press, London and New Jersey: Zed Books.

—— (1998) 'Gender and Transition in China and Vietnam'. Paper commissioned by the Swedish International Development Agency, Secretariat for Policy and Corporate Development/Economic and Social Analysis Division.

'Dagong mei zhi jia' bangongshi (1996) 'Zhi lai Jing dagong jiemeimen de yifeng gongkaixin' [Open letter to sisters who have come to the capital to work]. *'Nongjianü baishitong'* zazhishe. March.

Dahlerup, Drude (1986) 'Introduction', in Drude Dahlerup (ed.), *The New Women's Movement. Feminism and Political Power in Europe and the USA*. London: Sage Publications. 1–25.

—— (1986) 'Is the New Women's Movement Dead? Decline or Change of the Danish Movement', in Drude Dahlerup (ed.), *The New Women's Movement. Feminism and Political Power in Europe and the USA*. London: Sage Publications. 217–244.

—— (1993) 'From Movement Protest to State Feminism: the Women's Liberation Movement and Unemployment Policy in Denmark'. *NORA – Nordic Journal of Women's Studies*. Vol. 1, No. 1, 1–20.

—— (1998) *Rødstrømperne. Den danske Rødstrømpebevægelses udvikling, nytænkning og gennemslag 1970–1985* [The Redstockings. The development, innovative thinking and impact of the Danish Redstocking movement 1970–1985]. Copenhagen: Gyldendal.

—— (2000) 'Continuity and Waves in the Feminist Movement – a Challenge to Social Movement Theory', in Aino Saarinen, Hilda Rømer Christensen and Beatrice Halsaa (eds), *Women's Movements and Internationalisation: the 'Third Wave'?*. Oulu: Oulu University, 8–38.

Davin, Delia (1976). *Woman Work*. Oxford University Press: Oxford.

—— (1999) *Internal Migration in Contemporary China*. London: Macmillan.

DeLombard, Jeannine (1995) 'Femmenism', in Rebecca Walker (ed.), *To Be Real*. New York, London, Toronto, Sydney, Auckland: Anchor Books, 21–33.

Dikötter, Frank (1995) *Sex, Culture and Modernity in China: Medical Science and the Construction of Sexual Identities in the Early Republican Period*. London: Hurst & Company.

Ding Juan, Wang Ying, Yang Mei, Yang Jing, Zhou Jian, Miao Ye, Hou Zhiming and Dong Ou (1995, 1997) *Funü rexian 100 wen*. [The Women's Hotline – 100 questions]. Funü rexian congshu [Women's Hotline Collection]. Beijing: Haitun chubanshe.

Ding Ning (2000) *Nüxing yanzhong de waiyu* [Women's perspectives on extramarital relations], Beijing: Zhongguo wenlian chubanshe.

Ding Ning, Chen Xinxin, Li Hongtao, Hou Zhiming (eds), (1995) *Dang ni miandui lihun nanwen* [Facing the Dilemma of Divorce] Funü rexian congshu [Women's Hotline Collection] Beijing: Haitun chubanshe.

Du Fangqin (1997) 'My Way into Women's Studies'. *Asian Journal of Women's Studies*. Vol. 3, No 1, 133–160.

—— 2001. '"Maneuvering Fate" and "Following the Call"': Development and Prospects of Women's Studies', in Ping-Chun Hsiung, Maria Jaschok and Cecilia Milwertz with Red Chan (eds), *Chinese Women Organizing – Cadres, Feminists, Muslims, Queers.* Oxford: Berg.

Duan Yongqiang (ed.), (1987) *Waiguo nüquan yundong wenxuan* [Selections from the foreign feminist movement]. Beijing: Zhongguo funü chubanshe.

Edwards, Michael and David Hulme (1992) *Making a Difference: NGOs and Development in a Changing World.* London: Earthscan Publications.

Elliot, Dorinda (1998) 'Trying to Stand on Two Feet'. *Newsweek*, June 29, 36–37.

Erwin, Kathleen (2000) 'Heart-to-Heart, Phone-to-Phone', in Deborah S. Davis (ed.), *The Consumer Revolution in Urban China.* Berkeley, Los Angeles and London: University of California Press, 145–170.

Eyerman, Ron and Andrew Jamison (1991) *Social Movements. A Cognitive Approach.* Oxford: Polity Press.

—— (1998) *Music and Social Movements.* Cambridge: Cambridge University Press.

Evans, Harriet (1997) *Women and Sexuality in China.* Oxford: Polity Press.

Farrington, John and Anthony Bebbington with Kate Wellard and David J. Lewis (1993) *Reluctant Partners? Non-Governmental Organizations, the State and Sustainable Agricultural Development.* London and New York: Routledge.

Feng Yuan (2000) 'Claim rights: beyond the slogan and provisions', http:/ /www.philantrophy.org (downloaded 12 December).

Fennell, Vera and Lyn Jeffery (1992) *To Increase the Quality of Women. A Preliminary Assessment of Women's Studies in Beijing.* Beijing: Ford Foundation.

Ferguson, Ann (1997) 'Two Women's Studies Conferences in China: Report by an American Feminist Philosopher'. *Asian Journal of Women's Studies.* Vol. 3, No. 1, 161–184.

Ferree, Myra Marx and Patricia Yancey Martin (1995) 'Doing the Work of the Movement: Feminist Organisations', in Myra Marx Ferree and Patricia Yancey Martin (eds), *Feminist Organizations. Harvest of the New Women's Movement.* Philadelphia: Temple University Press, 3–23.

Flower, John and Pamela Leonard (1996) 'Community Values and State Cooption: Civil Society in the Sichuan Countryside', in Chris Hann and Elizabeth Dunn (eds), *Civil Society – Challenging Western Models.* London and New York: Routledge, 199–221.

Fog, Jette (1985) 'Om den følsomme fornuft og den fornuftige følsomhed' [On the sensitive rationality and the rational sensitivity]. *Psyke og Logos*, No. 6, 59–84.

Ford Foundation, Beijing (1995) *Interim Directory of Chinese Women's Organizations.* Beijing: Ford Foundation.

Forney, Matt (1996) 'Serve the People'. *Far Eastern Economic Review.* March 7, 28–29.

—— (1998) 'Voice of the People'. *Far Eastern Economic Review.* May 7, 10–12.

Frick, Heike, Mechthild Leutner and Nicola Spakowski (eds), (1995) *Frauenforschung in China: Analysen, Texte, Bibliographie.* München: Minerva Publikation.

Gao Mingye, Wang Xingjuan and Ding Ning (1997) '*Weicheng' nei de baoli – ouda* [Domestic Violence]. Funü rexian congshu [Women's Hotline Collection]. Beijing: Zhongyuan nongmin chubanshe.

Ge Youli and Susie Jolly (2001) 'East Meets West Feminist Translation Group: A Conversation between Two Participants', in Ping-Chun Hsiung, Maria Jaschok and Cecilia Milwertz with Red Chan (eds), *Chinese Women Organizing – Cadres, Feminists, Muslims, Queers.* Oxford: Berg.

Gilmartin, Christina (1990) 'Violence Against Women in Contemporary China', in Jonathan N. Lipman and Stevan Harrell (eds), *Violence in China,* New York: State University of New York Press, 203–221.

Gluck, Sherna Berger (1998) 'Whose Feminism, Whose History? Reflections on Excavating the History of (the) US Women's Movement(s)', in Nancy A. Naples (ed.), *Community Activism and Feminist Politics. Organizing Across Race, Class, and Gender.* New York and London: Routledge, 31–56.

Greenhalgh, Susan (1994) 'Controlling Births and Bodies in Village China'. *American Ethnologist* Vol. 21, No. 1, 3–30.

Gusfield, Joseph R. (1981) 'social Movements and Social Change: Perspectives of Linearity and Fluidity'. *Research on Social Movements, Conflict and Change.* Vol. 4, 317–39

Hann, Chris (1996) 'Introduction: Political Society and Civil Anthropology', in Chris Hann and Elizabeth Dunn (eds), *Civil Society – Challenging Western Models.* London and New York: Routledge, 1–26.

Hann, Chris and Elizabeth Dunn (eds), (1996) *Civil Society – Challenging Western Models.* London and New York: Routledge.

Hastrup, Kirsten (1992) 'Writing Ethnography. State of the Art', in Judith Okely and Helen Callaway (eds), *Anthropology and Autobiography.* London and New York. Routledge, 116–133.

He Xiaopei. 2001. 'Chinese Queer (*Tongzhi*) Women Organizing in the 1990s', in Ping-Chun Hsiung, Maria Jaschok and Cecilia Milwertz with Red Chan (eds), *Chinese Women Organizing – Cadres, Feminists, Muslims, Queers.* Oxford: Berg.

Hester, Marianne (2000) 'Domestic violence in China', in Jill Radford, Melissa Friedberg and Lynne Harne (eds), *Women, violence and strategies for action. Feminist research, policy and practice.* Buckingham and Philadelphia: Open University Press, 149–166.

Hongfeng funü xinli zixun fuwu zhongxin/The Maple Women's Psychological Counselling Center (1998) *Guanhuai nüxing, zhichi nüxing – Qingzhu Beijing hongfeng funü xinli zixun fuwu zhongxin chengli shizhounian* [Providing care and support for women – celebrating the 10th anniversary of the founding of the Maple Women's Psychological Counselling Centre, Beijing]. Beijing: Hongfeng funü xinli zixun fuwu zhongxin.

Honig, Emily and Gail Hershatter (1988) *Personal Voices. Chinese Women in the 1980's*. Stanford, California: Stanford University Press.

Hongjie (1995) 'Wo xiang dang laoban' [I want to be a manager], *Nongjianü baishitong* [Rural women knowing all], No. 7, 22–23.

Howell, Jude (1997a) 'Post-Beijing Reflections. Creating Ripples, but not Waves in China'. *Women's Studies International Forum*. Vol. 20, No. 2, 235–252.

—— (1997b) 'Political Transformation, Gender and Public Space'. Paper prepared for Political Transformation and Public Spaces Symposium, University of Westminster, 27 May.

Hsiung, Ping-Chun, Maria Jaschok and Cecilia Milwertz with Red Chan (eds), (2001) *Chinese Women Organizing – Cadres, Feminists, Muslims, Queers*. Oxford: Berg.

Hsiung, Ping-Chun and Yuk-Lin Renita Wong (1998) 'Jie Gui – Connecting the Tracks: Chinese Women's Activism Surrounding the 1995 World Conference on Women in Beijing'. *Gender and History*. Vol. 10, No. 3, 470–497.

Huang Hengyu, Ren Chunyan, Lü Qin, Li Hongtao, Ding Ning and Hou Zhiming (eds), (1995) *Zouchu ni xinling de wuqu* [Walking out of the erroneous zones of the soul] Funü rexian congshu (Women's Hotline Collection] Beijing: Haitun chubanshe.

Human Rights in China (1998) 'Bound and gagged: freedom of association in China further curtailed under new regulations'. Website release 13 November.

Jacka, Tamara (1990) 'Back to the Wok: Women and Employment in Chinese Industry in the 1980s'. *The Australian Journal of Chinese Affairs*. Issue 24 (July), 1–23.

Jaschok, Maria (1998) 'Chinese Educational Reforms and Feminist Praxis: On Ideals, Process and Paradigm', in Michael Agelasto and Bob Adamson (eds), *Higher Education in Post-Mao China*. Hong Kong: Hong Kong University Press, 321–343.

Jaschok, Maria, Cecilia Milwertz and Ping-Chun Hsiung (2001) 'Introduction', in Ping-Chun Hsiung, Maria Jaschok and Cecilia Milwertz with Red Chan (eds), (2001) *Chinese Women Organizing – Cadres, Feminists, Muslims, Queers*. Oxford: Berg, 3–21.

Jiang Wandi (1995) 'The Special Way of Chinese NGOs'. *NGO Forum on Women*. Saturday, September 2.

Johansson, Sten and Ola Nygren (1991) 'The Missing Girls of China: a New Demographic Account.' *Population and Development Review.* Vol. 17, No. 1 (March), 35–51.

Le Ping (1995a). *Xingsaorao dui zhiye funü de yingxiang ji qi duice yanjiu* [Research on the influence of sexual harassment on professional women and on policy measures]. Beijing: Zhongguo guanli kexue yanjiuyuan funü yanjiusuo.

—— (1995b) *The Influence of Sexual Harassment on Career Women and Research on Countermeasures.* Beijing: Zhongguo guanli kexue yanjiuyuan funü yanjiusuo.

Le Ping, Lü Xuejing, Dong Ou, Yang Jing, Tian Ying and Lü Qin (eds), (1995) *Hemu shenghuo zai tongyi kongjian* [Sharing a space harmoniously] Funü rexian congshu [Women's hotline collection]. Beijing: Haitun chubanshe.

Li Jianyong and Li Tao (1999) *Chengshi li ni you duo yuan* [How far away is the city – knowing all about job-hunting in the city], Shanghai: Shanghai kexue puji chubanshe.

Li Tao (1996) 'Tigao suzhi moqiu fazhan. "Dagong mei zhi jia" de renwu yu qiantu'. [Improve quality, strive for development – the tasks and future of the Migrant Women's Club]. Unpublished paper.

—— (1997) 'Hui jia' [Returning home]. *Zhongguo funübao* [China women's news]. 4 April, 3.

Li Xiaojiang (1989) *Nüren de chulu.* [Women's hope for the future] Shenyang: Liaoning renmin chubanshe.

—— (1991) 'Funü yanjiu zai Zhongguo de fazhan ji qi qianjing zhanwang' [The development and prospects of women's studies in China], in Li Xiaojiang and Tan Shen (eds), *Funü Yanjiu zai Zhongguo.* [Women's studies in China]. Henan: Henan renmin chubanshe, 3–22.

—— (1997) 'Shui shi Zhongguo funü NGO?' [Who are China's women's NGOs?], in Li Xiaojiang (ed.), *Guanyu nüren de dawen* [Responses to question on women]. Nanjing: Jiangsu renmin chubanshe, 68–80.

—— (2000) 'Gonggong kongjian de chuangzao' [Creating a public space], in Li Xiaojiang. (ed.), *Shen lin 'qi' jing* [Participating in the extraordinary]. Jiangsu: Jiangsu renmin chubanshe, 3–38.

Li Yaodong (ed.), (1992) *Zhongguo shehui tuanti yanjiu* [Research on Chinese social organizations]. Beijing: Zhongguo shehui chubanshe.

Li Yinhe, Lin Chun and Tan Shen (eds), (1997) *Funü zui manchang de geming* [Women's longest revolution]. Beijing: Sanlian chubanshe.

Liang Jun (1989) 'Mantan dangdai funü yao zou de lu' [A discussion of the paths of contemporary women], in Zhongyang renmin guangbo diantai 'Wujian banxiaoshi' (ed.), *Nüxing – hunyin – fuqin* [Women – marriage – fathers]. Beijing: Zhongguo guoji guangbo chubanshe, 1–39.

Lin Chun, Liu Bohong and Jin Yihong (1995a) 'Gender Equality in China: Between the State and the Market'. Paper presented at the International Symposium Chinese Women and Feminist Thought. June 21–24, 1995 in Beijing, 48–61.

—— (1995b) 'Toward A Chinese Feminism. A Personal Story' *Dissent.* Fall 1995, 477–485.

—— (1996) 'Citizenship in China: The Gender Politics of Social Transformation'. *Social Politics.* Summer/Fall, 278–290.

—— (1998) 'China', in Alison M. Jagger and Iris Marion Young (eds), *A Companion to Feminist Philosophy.* Malden, Massachusetts and Oxford: Blackwell Publishers,108–117.

Liu Bohong (ed.), (1998) *Meiguofunü ziwo baojian jingdian – women de shenti, women ziji* [Boston Women's Health Collective – Our Bodies Ourselves]. Beijing: Zhishi chubanshe.

Liu Dongxiao (1999) 'The Dialectic of 'Tizhinei' and 'Tizhi wai' – Institutional Heterogeneity and Social Change'. Unpublished manuscript.

Liu Guanghua (ed.), (1999) *Nüren jiedu ai – Zhongguo nüxing xinshiji de huisheng* [Women deconstructing love – echoes of women in the 20th century]. Beijing: Zhongguo chengshi chubanshe.

Liu Jinxiu (1991) '80 niandai funü minjian zuzhi de xingqi yu fazhan' [The rise and development of popular women's organizations in the 1980s], in Li Xiaojiang and Tan Shen (eds), *Funü yanjiu zai Zhongguo* [Women's studies in China]. Henan: Henan renmin chubanshe, 106–117.

Long Di (ed.), (1995) *Xiaonü ketang* [Girls' classes]. Beijing: Zhishi chubanshe.

Lønnå, Elisabeth (2000) 'Discussing waves in feminism', in Aino Saarinen, Hilda Rømer Christensen and Beatrice Halsaa (eds), *Women's Movements and Internationalisation: the 'Third Wave'?* Oulu: Oulu University, 39–51.

MacLeod, Lijia (1997) 'Wife-bashing comes into the spotlight'. *South China Morning Post.* 30 December, 13.

Mallee, Hein and Frank N. Pieke (eds), (1999) *Chinese Migrants and European Chinese: Perspectives on Internal and International Migration.* Richmond, Surrey: Curzon Press.

Margolis, Diane Rothbard (1993) 'Women's Movements Around the World: Cross-Cultural Comparison'. *Gender and Society.* Vol. 7, No. 3 (September), 379–399.

Milwertz, Cecilia (1996) 'Et vindue til verden' [A window on the world], in Liss Hansen (ed.), *Kvindeviljer – om græsrødder, netværk og FN-konferencer* [Women's determination – on grassroots, networks and UN conferences]. Copenhagen: Kvindernes U-landsudvalg, 20–25.

—— (1997) *Accepting Population Control – Urban Chinese Women and the One-child Family Policy.* Richmond: Curzon Press.

—— (2000a) 'The 1990s Women's Movement in Beijing – Ideology, Values and Practice', in Aino Saarinen, Hilda Rømer Christensen and Beatrice Halsaa (eds), *Women's Movements and Internationalisation: the 'Third Wave'?* Oulu: Oulu University, 60–72.

—— (2000b) 'Organizing Rural Migrant Women in Beijing', in Jane Drake, Sue Ledwith and Roberta Woods (eds), *Women and the City. Visibility and Voice in Urban Space.* London: Macmillan, 174–188.

Milwertz, Cecilia and Qi Wang (1995) *Fra Maosko til Laksko.* [From cloth shoes to patent leather]. Copenhagen: Kvindernes U-landsudvalg.

Min Dongchao (1998) 'Translation as crossing borders: a case study of the translations of the word "feminism" into Chinese'. Unpublished paper.

Molyneux, Maxine (1985) 'Mobilization Without Emancipation? Women's Interests, the State, and Revolution in Nicaragua'. *Feminist Studies.* Vol. 11, No. 2 (Summer), 227–254.

Morgan, Robin (1984) 'Introduction. Planetary Feminism: The Politics of the 21st Century', in Robin Morgan (ed.), *Sisterhood is Global.* Penguin Books, 1–37.

Morris, Aldon D. (1992) Political Consciousness and Collective Action', in Aldon D. Morris and Carol McClurg Mueller (eds), *Frontiers in Social Movement Theory.* New Haven and London: Yale University Press, 351–73.

Moser, Caroline O.N. (1993) *Gender Planning and Development.* London and New York: Routledge.

Mueller, Carol McClurg (1987) 'Collective Consciousness, Identity Transformation, and the Rise of Women in Public Office in the United States', in Mary Fainsod Katzenstein and Carol McClurg Mueller (eds), *The Women's Movements in the United States and Western Europe: Consciousness, Political Opportunity, and Public Policy.* Philadelphia: Temple University Press.

Mufson, Steven (1998) 'Ex-Devotee of Mao Devotes Her Career to Women / A Risk-Taker Seeks Solutions for Sisters'. *The Washington Post.* Thursday, June 18, A30.

Naples, Nancy A. (1998a) 'Introduction', in Nancy A. Naples (ed.), *Community Activism and Feminist Politics.* New York and London: Routledge, 1–27.

—— (1998b) 'Women's Community Activism', in Nancy A. Naples (ed.), *Community Activism and Feminist Politics.* New York and London: Routledge, 327–349.

Naples, Nancy A. (ed.), (1998c) *Community Activism and Feminist Politics.* New York and London: Routledge.

Narayan, Uma (1997) *Dislocating Cultures.* New York and London: Routledge.

Ng, Man Lun and Erwin J. Haeberle (1997) *Sexual Behaviour in Modern China.* New York: Continuum.

Nongjianü baishitong [Rural women knowing all] (n.d., approximately 1997) Brochure in Chinese and English.

Nongjianü baishitong [Rural women knowing all] and Tianjin shifan daxue funü yanjiu zhongxin [Centre for Women's Studies, Tianjin Normal University] (eds), (1995) *Dangdai nongcun funü fazhan yu duice* [The development and strategy of contemporary rural women]. Beijing: Zhongguo funü chubanshe.

Nussbaum, Martha (1995) 'Women and Cultural Universals'. Paper presented at the International Symposium Chinese Women and Feminist Thought. Beijing, 21–24 June, 62–82.

Omvedt, Gail (1993) *Reinventing Revolution – New Social Movements and the Socialist Tradition in India.* M.E.Sharpe: New York, London.

Palmer, Stephen, Wang Xingjuan and Xiao-Ming Jia (1998) 'Counselling in China: Telephone 'hotlines''. *Counselling Psychology Review.* Vol. 13, No. 2, May, 21–25.

Pearsall, Judy (1998) *The New Oxford Dictionary of English.* Oxford: Clarendon Press.

Pei, Minxin (1999) 'Rights and resistance', in Elizabeth J. Perry and Mark Selden (eds), *Chinese Society.* London and New York: Routledge, 20–40.

Perry, Elizabeth J. (1995) 'Introduction' (to Part III Urban Spaces), in Deborah S. Davis, Richard Kraus, Barry Naughton, and Elizabeth J. Perry (eds), *Urban Spaces in Contemporary China.* Washington/Cambridge: Woodrow Wilson Center Press and Cambridge University Press, 297–301.

Perry, Susan (2001) 'Between a Rock and a Hard Place: Women's Non-Governmental Activity in China', in Susan Perry and Celeste Schenck (eds), *Eye to Eye. Women Practising Development Across Cultures.* London and New York: Zed Books.

Pi Xiaoming (1991) 'Jiating baoli – baipishu' [Domestic Violence – Whitebook]. *Zhongguo funü* [Chinese Women]. No. 12, 20–22.

Pietilä, Hilkka and Jeanne Vickers ((1990) 1996) *Making Women Matter. The Role of the United Nations.* Zed Books: London and New Jersey.

Privat, Pascal with Michelle Litvin (1990) 'Hope HotLine, May I Help You?' *Newsweek.* 16 July, 34.

Pun Ngai (1999) 'Becoming *Dagongmei*: the Politics of Identity and Difference in Reform China'. *The China Journal.* No. 42, July, 1–18.

Qiao Genmei (1999) *Xuehui guanxin ni ziji – funü shengyu jiankang* [Learn to care for yourself – knowing all about reproductive health]. Shanghai: Shanghai kexue puji chubanshe.

Quanguo fulian funü yanjiusuo [Women's Studies Institute of China] (ed.), (1995) '*Funü yanjiu zai Zhongguo*' zhuanti yantaohui lunwenji. [A collection of theses on 'Women's Studies in China']. Prepared for the United Nations' Fourth World Conference on Women, NGO Forum 1995. Beijing: Quanguo fulian funü yanjiusuo.

Raab, Michaela (1997) 'Non-governmental social development groups in China. Summary of a study commissioned by the Ford Foundation (August–December 1996)'. Beijing: Ford Foundation.

Racioppi, Linda and Katherine O'Sullivan See (1995) 'Organizing Women before and after the Fall: Women's Politics in the Soviet Union and Russia'. *Signs: Journal of Women in Culture and Society.* Vol. 20, No. 4, 818–850.

Ren Chunyan and Xu Xiuyu (1997) *Shenbian de yangying* [The shadow surrounding you – sexual harassment]. Funü rexian congshu [Women's hotline collection]. Beijing: Zhongyuan nongmin chubanshe.

Rosander, Eva Evers (1997) 'Women in Groups in Africa: Female Associational Patterns in Senegal and Morocco', in Dawn Chatty and Annika Rabo (eds), *Organizing Women – Formal and Informal Women's Groups in the Middle East.* Oxford and New York: Berg, 101–23.

Roseneil, Sasha (1995) *Disarming Patriarchy. Feminism and Political Action at Greenham.* Buckhingham and Philadelphia: Open University Press.

—— (1996) 'Transgressions and Transformations. Experience, counsciousness and identity at Greenham', in Nickie Charles and Felicia Huges-Freeland (eds), *Practising Feminism. Identity, Difference, Power.* London and New York: Routledge, 86–108.

Roseneil, Sasha and Julie Seymore (1999) 'Practising Identities: Power and Resistance', in Sasha Roseneil and Julie Seymore (eds), *Practicing Identities: Power and Resistance.* Hampshire and London: Macmillan, 1–10.

Rupp, Laila (1994) 'Constructing Internationalism: The Case of Transnational Women's Organisations, 1888–1945. *American Historical Review.* December, 1571–1600.

—— (1997) *Worlds of Women. The Making of an International Women's Movement.* Princeton, New Jersey: Princeton University Press.

Ryan, Barbara (1992) *Feminism and the Women's Movement.* New York and London: Routledge.

Sandoval, Chela (1991) 'U.S. Third World Feminism: The Theory and Method of Oppositional Consiousness in the Postmodern World'. *Genders.* No. 10, Spring, 1–24.

Sausmikat, Nora (2001) 'NGO, Frauen und China', *Asien – Deutsche Zeitschrift für Politik, Wirtschaft und Kultur,* No. 80, July, 81–92.

Shehui tuanti dengji guanli tiaoli (1998) Regulations on the Registration and Management of Social Organisations. Adopted by the State Council on 25 September 1998 and promulgated by Premier Zhu Rongji on 25 October 1998.

Sigley, Gary and Elaine Jeffreys (1999) 'On "Sex" and "Sexuality" in China: A Conversation with Pan Suiming'. *Bulletin of Concerned Asian Scholars,* Vol. 31, No. 1, 50–58.

Smith, Bonnie (ed.), (2000) *Global Feminisms since 1945.* London and New York: Routledge.

Solinger, Dorothy J. (1998) 'Job Categories and Employment Channels Among the "Floating Population"', in Greg O'Leary (ed.), *Adjusting to Capitalism. Chinese Workers and the State*. New York and London: M.E. Sharpe, 3–47.

Spakowski, Nicola (2001) 'The Internationalization of China's Women's Studies', *Berliner China Hefte*, 20, May, 79–100.

Staggenborg, Suzanne (1995) 'Can Feminist Organisations Be Effective?', in Myra Marx Ferree and Patricia Yancey Martin (eds), *Feminist Organizations*. Philadelphia: Temple University Press, 339–355.

Stearns, Lisa (1996) *Promoting Gender Equality in China. A background paper for Sida*. Stockholm: Sida Policy Jämställdhetsenheten (Equality unit).

Stienstra, Deborah (2000) 'Dancing resistance from Rio to Beijing', in Marianne H. Marchand and Anne Sisson Runyan (eds), *Gender and Global Restructuring*. London and New York: Routledge, 209–224.

Sun Jin (1999) *Bang ni da guansi – nongjia falü zhishi* [Help in lawsuits – knowing all about the law], Shanghai: Shanghai kexue puji chubanshe.

Swidler, Ann (1995) 'Cultural Power and Social Movements', in Hank Johnston and Bert Klandermans (eds), *Social Movements and Culture*. London: University College, 25–40.

Tan Lin and Peng Xizhe (2000) 'China's Female Population', in Peng Xizhi with Guo Zhigang (eds), *The Changing Population of China*. Oxford: Blackwell Publishers.

Tan Shen (1991) 'Dui jinnian funü yanjiu xianxiang de shehuixue kaocha' [A sociological study of the phenomena of women's studies during the latest years], in Li Xiaojiang and Tan Shen (eds), *Funü yanjiu zai Zhongguo* [Women's studies in China]. Henan: Henan renmin chubanshe, 23–42. Translated in a shorter version to: Tan Shen (1993) 'Women's Studies in China: A General Survey'. *Copenhagen Discussion Papers*. No. 19. (April).

—— (1995) 'Biange zhong funü de liang ge shang zhong da wenti' [Two major issues emerging in the reform of today's China]. Paper presented at the International Symposium Chinese Women and Feminist Thought. Beijing, 21–24 June, 161–172.

—— (1997) 'Nongcun laodongli liudong de xingbie chayi' [Sexual difference in migrant rural labour]. *Shehuixue yanjiu* [Sociological research], No. 1, 42–47.

Tang Can (1996) 'Xingsaorao: chengshi wailai nümingong de shuangchong shenfen yu qishi' [Sexual harassment: migrant female workers' double status and discrimination]. *Shehuixue yanjiu* [Sociological research]. No. 4, 116–125.

Taylor, Verta and Nancy Whittier (1995) 'Analytical Approaches to Social Movement Culture: The Culture of the Women's Movement', in Hank Johnston and Bert Klandermans (eds), *Social Movements and Culture*. London: University College, 163–187.

Tong Xin (1999) 'The Production and Reproduction of Unequal Gender Relations – an Analysis of Domestic Violence in China', in Lisa Stearns (ed.), *Chinese Women's Rights.* Working Paper No. 10, Oslo: Institutt for Menneskerettigheter (Norwegian Institute of Human Rights), 42–56.

Tu Ping (1993) 'Wo guo chusheng yinger xingbiebi wenti tansuo' [An exploration of the sex ratio at birth in China]. *Renkou Yanjiu.* No. 1, 6–13.

Walker, Tony (1993) 'Chinese Men Embrace Divorce'. *World Press Review.* October, 48.

Wan Yanhai (2000) 'A Strange Love Affair'. China Rights Forum. No. 1 (Winter), 4–10.

Wan Shanping (1988) 'The Emergence of Women's Studies in China'. *Women's Studies International Forum.* Vol. 11, No. 5, 455–64.

Wang Dingbi (1997) 'Weile haizi' [For the Sake of Children]. *Nongjianü Baihitong* [Rural women knowing all]. No. 1, 19.

Wang Fengxian (1996) *Nüren – guizhe zhanzhe* [Woman – kneeling, standing]. Beijing: Longmen shuju.

Wang Haiying (1995) 'Haishi jiaxiang hao' [Home is best]. *Nongjianü Baishitong* [Rural women knowing all]. No. 8, 10–11.

Wang Kaijie, Ma Huilan, Tian Yao and Wang Fu'e (1997) *Shui neng gei wo gongdao – falü* [Who can give me justice – the law]. Funü rexian congshu [Women's hotline collection]. Beijing: Zhongyuan nongmin chubanshe.

Wang Xingjuan. (n.d.) 'Beijing chengqu jiating baoli zhuangkuang yu duice yanjiu' [Research on the situation of domestic violence and countermeasures in Beijing city districts]. Unpublished report.

—— (1995) 'I am Busy Raising Funds', in Wong Yuen Ling (ed.), *Reflections and Resonance: Studies of Chinese Women Involved in International Preparatory Activities for the 1995 NGO Forum on Women.* Beijing: Ford Foundation, 11–17.

—— (1999a) 'Yiwei lixie zhishi nüxing de zhuiqiu' [The pursuit of a retired woman intellectual], in Liu Guanghua (ed.), *Nüren jiedu ai – Zhongguo nüxing xinshiji de huisheng* [Women Deconstructing Love – Echoes of Women in the 20th Century], Beijing: Zhongguo chengshi chubanshe, 318–331.

—— (1999b) 'Why are Beijing Women Beaten by Their Husbands?: A Case Analysis of Family Violence in Beijing'. *Violence Against Women.* Vol. 5, Issue 12, 1493–1504.

—— (1999c) 'Zai Zhongguo shehui bianqian zhong – yige minjian funü zuzhi de jiase yu fazhan.' [English version: During the Social Change in China: The Role and Development of a Non-governmental Women's Organization]. Paper presented at the Workshop 'Women Organizing in China, the University of Oxford, July.

—— (2000) 'Yige funü caogen zuzhi de shengzhang' [The growth of a women's grassroots organization], in Li Xiaojiang (ed.), *Shen lin'qi' jing* [Participating in the Extraordinary]. Jiangsu: Jiangsu renmin chubanshe, 237–273.

Wang Xingjuan and Wang Fengxian (eds), (2000) *Dianhua xinli zixun de lilun yu shixian* [Theory and Practice of the Telephone Psychological Counselling]. Beijing: Kunlun chubanshe.

Wang Xingjuan, Xu Xiuyu and Wang Ling (1995, 1997) *Rang xingshenghuo meiman he xie.* [Attaining a fulfilling and harmonious sexual life]. Funü rexian congshu [Women's hotline collection] Beijing: Haitun chubanshe.

Wang Yongchen (ed.), (1995) *Voices of Women – Funü dubai.* Haikou: Hainan Publishing House.

Wang Zheng (1997) 'Maoism, feminism, and the UN conference on women: Women's Studies research in contemporary China'. *Journal of Women's History,* Vol. 8, No. 4, 126–152.

—— (1999) *Women in the Chinese Enlightenment. Oral and Textual Histories.* Berkeley, Los Angeles and Oxford: University of California Press.

—— (2000) 'Gender, employment and women's resistance', in Elizabeth J. Perry and Mark Selden (eds), *Chinese Society.* London and New York: Routledge, 62–82.

Wesoky, Sharon (1998) 'Globalization, Social Movement Forms, and Non-democratic Contexts: The Case of the Beijing Women's Movement'. Paper prepared for the 50th Annual Meeting of the Association for Asian Studies, March 26–29.

—— (1999) 'Symbiotic Discourses and the Contemporary Chinese Women's Movement', Paper presented at the Workshop 'Women Organizing in China', University of Oxford, July.

West, Lois A. (1999) 'The United Nations Women's Conferences and Feminist Politics', in Mary K. Meyer and Elisabeth Prügl (eds), *Gender Politics in Global Governance.* Lanham, Boulder, New York and Oxford: Rowman & Litllefield Publishers, 177–272.

White, Gordon, Jude Howell and Shang Xiaoyuan (1996) *In Search of Civil Society.* Oxford: Clarendon Press.

Whiting, Susan (1989) *The Non-governmental Sector in China. A Preliminary Report.* Beijing: The Ford Foundation.

Women's Research Institute (n.d.) *A Creation of China: Hotline for Women, Specialists' Hotline for Women.* (Zhongguo de shouchuang: Funü rexian, funü zhuanjia rexian). Beijing: Women's Research Institute, China Academy of Management Science.

Women's Research Institute, China Academy of Management Science) (1994). *What progress we have made 1988–1994.* Beijing: Women's Research Institute, China Academy of Management Science.

—— (1995) *The Progress We Have Made 1988–1995*. Beijing: Women's Research Institute, China Academy of Management Science.

Wong Yuen Ling (ed.), (1995) *Reflections and Resonance: Studies of Chinese Women Involved in International Preparatory Activities for the 1995 NGO Forum on Women*. Beijing: the Ford Foundation.

World Health Organization (1999) *Figures and Facts about Suicide*. Geneva: Department of Mental Health, WHO.

Wu Qing (1999) 'What I Know about Gender and Development', in Marilyn Porter and Ellen Judd (eds), *Feminists Doing Development*. London and New York: Zed Books, 57–69.

Xie Lihua (1995a) 'Guniang, nimen weishenme jin cheng' [Girls, why do you move to the cities]. *Nongjianü baishitong* [Rural women knowing all]. No. 1, 4–7.

—— (1995b) 'Women de guwen – Wu Qing' [Our Advisor – Wu Qing]. *Nongjianü baishitong*. [Rural Women Knowing All]. Number 8, 4–6.

—— (1995c) '"Nongjianü baishitong zazhi" de ban kan sixiang he faxing celüe' [The management ideology and distribution strategy of the magazine rural women knowing all], in *Nongjianü baishitong* and Tianjin shifan daxue funü yanjiu zhongxin (eds), *Dangdai nongcun funü fazhan yu duice* [The development and strategy of contemporary rural women]. Beijing: Zhongguo funü chubanshe, 221–227.

—— (1995d) 'Introduction', in Long Di (ed.), *Xiaonü ketang* [Girls' classes]. Beijing: Zhishi chubanshe, 1–6.

Xie Lihua and Song Meiya (eds), (1999a) *Chengshi li ni you duo yuan* [How far away is the city]. Shanghai: Shanghai kexue puji chubanshe.

—— (eds), (1999b) *Zhongguo nongcun funü zishabaogao* [Report on women's suicides in rural China]. Guizhou; Guizhou renmin chubanshe.

Xiong Lei (1997) 'Media Situation and Women in Media'. Paper presented at the Regional Conference on Women and the Media, World Association of Christian Communication and ISIS International, Manila, July–August.

Yang, Mayfair Meihui (1994) *Gifts, Favours and Banquets*. Ithaca & London: Cornell University Press.

Yang Mei (1997a) 'Women's Hotlines in China and their Features.' Paper presented at a meeting held by Kvindernes U-landsudvalg [KULU – Women and Development], Copenhagen, 22 May.

—— (1997b) *Funü rexian zixun shouce* [Women's hotline counselling handbook] Beijing: Zhongguo qingnian chubanshe.

Yi Nuo, Jin Xi and Chun Yan (1995) '*Wo shi Zhongguo danshen nüxing*' ['I am China's single woman'], Beijing: Guangming ribao chubanshe.

Zhang Jufang (1999) *Xiaokang bu shi meng –nongjia zhifu lu* [Prosperity is not a dream – knowing all about money-making], Shanghai: Shanghai kexue puji chubanshe.

Zhang Junzuo (1994) 'Development in Chinese Reality: Rural Women's Organizations in China'. *The Journal of Communist Studies and Transition Politics*. Vol. 10, No. 4, December, 71–92.

Zhang Naihua (2001) 'searching for 'Authentic' NGOs: The NGO Discourse and Women's Organizations in China', in Ping-Chun Hsiung, Maria Jaschok and Cecilia Milwertz with Red Chan (eds), *Chinese Women Organizing – Cadres, Feminists, Muslims, Queers*. Oxford: Berg.

Zhang Naihua with Wu Xu (1995) 'Discovering the Positive Within the Negative: The Women's Movement in a Changing China', in Amrita Basu (ed.), *The Challenge of Local Feminisms: Women's Movements in Global Perspective*. Boulder, San Francisco, Oxford: Westview Press, 25–57.

Zhao Shilin (1995) 'Ku la suan tian nan sushuo' [Bitter, hot, sour, sweet is difficult to tell], *Nongjianü baishitong* [Rural women knowing all], No. 2, 4–7.

Zheng Rongchang, Fei Lipeng, Liu Huaqing and Zhang Yanping (2000) *Zhongguo nongcun funü qinggan zishu* [Personal accounts of Chinese rural women]. Guizhou: Guizhou renmin chubanshe.

Zhongguo guanli kexue yanjiuyuan funü yanjiusuo [Women's Research Institute, China Academy of Management Science] (n.d.) *Xuehui yong falü baohu ni ziji* [Learning how to protect yourself by using the law]. Beijing: Zhongguo guanli kexue yanjiuyuan funü yanjiusuo.

—— (1990a) 'Zhongguo shehui funü jiuye qushi yanjiu' [Trends in the employment of women in China – part one]. *Funü gongzuo* [Woman Work]. 6, 17–20.

—— (1990b) 'Zhongguo shehui funü jiuye qushi yanjiu' [Trends in the employment of women in China – part two]. *Funü gongzuo* [Woman Work]. 7, 22–25.

—— (1994a) *Zouguo de lu 1988–1994* [Progress report 1988–1994]. Beijing: Zhongguo guanli kexue yanjiuyuan funü yanjiusuo.

—— (1994b) *Dangdai Zhongguo nüxing de kunrao* [The perplexed state of women in contemporary China]. Beijing: Zhongguo guanli kexue yanjiuyuan funü yanjiusuo.

—— (1995a) *Zouguo de lu 1988–1995* [Progress report 1988–1995]. Beijing: Zhongguo guanli kexue yanjiuyuan funü yanjiusuo.

—— (1995b) *Funü qunti yu shehui qiuzhu* [Women's group and social support]. Folder prepared for the United Nations Fourth World Conference on Women, NGO Forum workshop. The Women's Research Institute, China Academy of Management Science: Beijing.

Zhonghua quanguo funü lianhehui funü yanjiusuo and Shaanxisheng funü lianhehui yanjiusuo [Research Institute of the All China Women's Federation and Research Office of Shannxi Province Women's Federation] (ed.), (1991). *Zhongguo funü tongji ziliao (1949–1989)*. [Statistics on Chinese Women (1949–1989)]. Beijing: Zhongguo tongji chubanshe.

Zhongyang renmin guangbo diantai 'Wujian banxiaoshi' (ed.), (1989) *Nüxing – Hunyin – Fuqin.* [Women – marriage – fathers]. Beijing: Zhongguo guoji guangbo chubanshe.

Zhu Chuzhu (1990) 'Gaige beijingxia de Zhongguo nüxing renkou.' [China's female population during the reforms], in Wu Cangping (ed.), *Gaige kaifang yu renkou fazhan.* [Reforms and population development]. Shenyang: Liaoning daxue chubanshe, 272–283.

Zhu Chuzhu, Li Shuzhuo, Qiu Changrong, Hu Ping and Jing Anrong (eds), (1997) *Jihua shengyu dui Zhongguo funü de shuangmian xingxiang* [The Dual Effects of the Family Planning Program on Chinese Women]. Xi'an: Xi'an Jiaotong University Press.

Index

The Nordic Institute of Asian Studies (NIAS) is funded by the governments of Denmark, Finland, Iceland, Norway and Sweden via the Nordic Council of Ministers, and works to encourage and support Asian studies in the Nordic countries. In so doing, NIAS has been publishing books since 1969, with more than one hundred titles produced in the last decade.

Nordic Council of Ministers